PREACHING
WITH
PASSION

PREACHING WITH PASSION

Alex Montoya

kregel
PUBLICATIONS

Grand Rapids, MI 49501

Preaching with Passion

© 2000 by Alex Montoya

Published by Kregel Publications, a division of Kregel, Inc., P.O. Box 2607, Grand Rapids, MI 49501. Kregel Publications provides trusted, biblical publications for Christian growth and service. Your comments and suggestions are valued.

For more information about Kregel Publications, visit our web site: www.kregel.com

Library of Congress Cataloging-in-Publication Data
Montoya, Alex D.
Preaching with passion / Alex Montoya.
    p.   cm.
Includes bibliographical references.
1. Preaching. I. Title.
BV4211.2.M64   2000   251—dc21   00-035727

ISBN 0-8254-3346-0

Printed in the United States of America

1 2 3 4 5 / 04 03 02 01 00

Contents

Foreword

D. Martyn Lloyd-Jones said preaching is logic on fire. He meant that good preaching must bring together both well-reasoned biblical content and intense passion. Too many preachers miss one side or the other of the equation. There is certainly no shortage of preachers today who are all emotion and no content; I have addressed this imbalance in several of my books.

In this book, however, Alex Montoya addresses the opposite kind of imbalance—preachers whose content is just fine, but whose delivery is flat and passionless, more befitting the usual caricature of a classroom lecture than a prophetic message from almighty God.

Such preachers usually do not even realize the damage they do to the cause of truth. They may truly love the Word of God and have a high regard for sound doctrine, but what their dispassionate delivery actually communicates is apathy and indifference. In the end, they undermine the very work they believe they are called to advance. The world (and the church) would be better off without such preaching.

I have often said that if a man is unable to be passionate about the Word of God, he has no business preaching. If someone can stand in the pulpit and manage to make the Word of the living God sound dry and dull, that person ought to sit down and let someone else preach.

This is true even if he possesses top academic credentials; one's educational achievements alone cannot qualify that person to preach.

Mere logic without the fire of passion is far from the biblical ideal for preaching.

In fact, I'm convinced that even in the most sound and solid Bible churches today, much of what is labeled preaching is not that at all. Turn off the overhead, eliminate the Power-Point presentation, stop passing out the fill-in-the-blank outlines, and let the man of God proclaim the truth with genuine, heartfelt fervor, energized by the Spirit's unction. *That* is preaching.

This is no argument against training or preparation. Good preaching occurs when the well-trained mind—filled with knowledge, skilled at clarity, motivated by love for the truth, and energized by the Holy Spirit—speaks powerfully to people. The true preacher is never content with informing his people about a few academic matters. He wants to overwhelm them with clear and powerful exposition of the Word so that they feel the impact of God's truth at the most fundamental level.

Perhaps no one is better qualified to write about passionate preaching than Alex Montoya. He preaches as he lives his life—with a burning passion for the truth. Alex has been a good friend and faithful colaborer for many years. All who know him agree that his passion is infectious. Here's hoping this book will start an epidemic.

JOHN MACARTHUR

Introduction

I solemnly charge you in the presence of God and of Christ Jesus, who is to judge the living and the dead, and by His appearing and His kingdom: preach the word; be ready in season and out of season; reprove, rebuke, exhort, with great patience and instruction. For the time will come when they will not endure sound doctrine; but wanting to have their ears tickled, they will accumulate for themselves teachers in accordance to their own desires; and will turn away their ears from the truth, and will turn aside to myths. But you, be sober in all things, endure hardship, do the work of an evangelist, fulfill your ministry.

—2 Timothy 4:1–5

A preacher's task is to preach the Word! That is his job description.[1] The preacher is to be a faithful proclaimer of God's Word. Paul reminds Timothy of this awesome responsibility in 2 Timothy 4:1–5:

- A solemn charge: *In the presence of God.*
- A simple charge: *Preach the Word.*
- A ceaseless charge: *Preach . . . in season and out of season.*
- A serious charge: *Reprove, rebuke, exhort.*
- A sober charge: *Be sober in all things.*

9

In our struggle to be effective, contemporary preachers, we are tempted to avoid the charge or certain aspects of it. The lure of the crowd and of popularity can tempt us to compromise our call to *"preach the Word."* Too easily we make merchandise of the divine message and sell it cheaply to the fickle crowds. The church at large has no lack of window-shopping hearers who seek peddlers of the Word who will be content with simply pleasing the ear instead of changing the heart. Indeed, we preach in difficult times, and all of us preachers know it.

The fickle crowd needs a faithful preacher who will meet the charge Paul delivered to Timothy. But the crowd is not just fickle; it is also apathetic, listless, lifeless, and wetted down with the materialistic dew of the day. Such a people need preaching that connects with them, preaching that can awaken them from a spiritual stupor. *Such people need passionate preaching.*

Most of us are delivering the goods, as they say. We are preaching the Word faithfully. We stay tied to the text, preaching sound expositional messages. Yet we find our churches unresponsive and listless. For many of us, the congregation grows smaller with each passing year.

The problem is with neither the content of the sermon nor our methodology; rather, the problem lies with our delivery of the sermon. The problem is not *what* we say; it is *how* we say it. Our sermons lack passion.

The Need for Passion

The fact is that many of us simply preach sermons, not the Word of God. We preach the exegesis, not the divine oracle. We preach (sometimes read) crafted, alliterated manuscripts instead of the living Word. We are biblical, but the Word has been deadened by a lifeless delivery or a hampering style.

Our sermons need to come alive. They need to speak from the heart as well as from the head. They need to burn through our being and descend upon the lives of our hearers. *Passionate preaching is heart preaching.* Jerry Vines says, "We need a return to heart preaching. Perhaps some would use other terminology. Perhaps you would prefer the term *sincerity*. Or maybe you like the word *earnestness*. Whatever you choose to call it, we desperately need it!"[2]

The empty churches are due not so much to an absence of ability or a lack of desire to hear the truth as with an absolute boredom brought about by passionless preaching. Our people are screaming at us from the silent, empty pews!

Preaching longer sermons only prolongs the agony. I teach homiletics at the Master's Seminary. In one of these classes, our students are required to preach ten thirty-minute sermons. After one exceptionally boring sermon, as I commented on the ordeal, the student spoke up, "It would have been better if I had more time to preach." "No!" I responded. *"It would have only prolonged the agony!"* A short sermon is not a sign of shallowness (consider the Sermon on the Mount), nor is a long sermon a sign of depth!

We need passion in our preaching. The conservative, biblical preacher has to be most aware of the balance between solid exposition and the passionate delivery of that exposition. How we deliver the sermon is as important as what we deliver. The people whom we serve are in need of a word from the Lord. The living Word must show through a living preacher to a soul in need of life. Let us consider carefully this element as we preach.

> ## *"How we deliver the sermon is as important as what we deliver."*

I was refreshed to read what the great expositor Martyn Lloyd-Jones thought about this issue. Here is what he says:

> This element of pathos and of emotion is, to me, a very vital one. It is what has been so seriously lacking in the present century, and perhaps especially among Reformed people. We tend to lose our balance and to become over-intellectual, indeed almost to despise the element of feeling and emotion. We are such learned men, we have such a grasp of the Truth,

that we tend to despise feeling. The common herd, we feel, are emotional and sentimental, but they have no understanding![3]

The same sentiment is expressed by Geoffry Thomas in a chapter called "Powerful Preaching," when he acknowledges,

One of the great perils that face preachers of the Reformed faith is the problem of hyper-intellectualism, that is, the constant danger of lapsing into a purely cerebral form of proclamation, which falls exclusively upon the intellect. Men become obsessed with doctrine and end up as brain-oriented preachers. . . . The problem is universal.[4]

I must remind myself that God called me to *preach the Word*, not to deliver a lecture or an address, and not to read a manuscript for scholars. What a wake-up call!

Passion Is the Essence of Preaching

Passion is the power, the drive, the energy, the life in the delivery of the sermon. Without passion, the sermon becomes a lecture, an address, or a moral speech. If there is no passion, there is no preaching. W. A. Criswell, the famous Baptist preacher, states, "The sermon is no essay to be read for optional opinion, for people to casually consider. It is confrontation with Almighty God. It is to be delivered with a burning passion, in the authority of the Holy Spirit."[5] Listen to Criswell again:

You cannot read the New Testament without sensing that the preachers were electrified by the power of the Gospel and swept off their feet by the wonder of the great revelation which had been committed to their trust. There is something wrong if a man charged with the greatest news in the world can be listless and rigid and dull. Who is going to believe that the glad tidings brought by the preacher means literally more than anything else on earth if they are presented with no verve or fire or attack, and if the man himself is apathetic, uninspired, afflicted with spiritual coma in unsaying by his attitude what he says in words?[6]

Preaching is passionate because it deals with the very nature of God and the expression of His love for humanity. The attitude in the study and the attitude in the pulpit are similar yet different. The study is the discovery of the truth, and the pulpit is the sharing of this truth. The simmering of the week boils over in the pulpit on Sunday. How can we preach such magnificent truths as though they were common and mundane? Hence,

> What is preaching? Logic on fire! Eloquent reason! Are these contradictions? Of course they are not. Reason concerning this Truth ought to be mightily eloquent, as you see it in the case of the Apostle Paul and others. It is theology on fire. And a theology which does not take fire, I maintain, is a defective theology; or at least the man's understanding of it is defective. Preaching is theology coming through a man who is on fire. A true understanding and experience of the Truth must lead to this. I say again that a man who can speak about these things dispassionately has no right whatsoever to be in a pulpit and should never be allowed to enter one.[7]

Every preacher should heed that warning. He will save himself and his people much grief.

A preacher happened to glance at his audience and noticed an older gentleman swooning under his oration. He said to the little boy sitting next to the sleeping saint, "Little fellow, would you mind waking your grandfather?" The boy responded, "Why don't you do it? You put him to sleep!" Well said! If we put them to sleep, we should also awaken them. Over the years, my greatest fear has been that I would be a dull, boring preacher. How can so many of us drone away in our pulpits while our audiences sleep away?

We have too many dull, boring preachers in our pulpits. Some of these are very godly men, but they are dull nevertheless. Godliness is a requirement for all leaders, but passionate preaching is an added requirement for all *preachers*. I like what Charles Spurgeon says:

> We must regard the people as the wood and the sacrifice, well wetted a second and a third time by the cares of the week, upon which, like the prophet, we must pray down the fire from heaven. A dull minister creates a dull audience. You cannot expect the office-bearers and members of the church to travel by steam if their own chosen pastor still drives the old broad-wheeled wagon.[8]

And speaking of boring preachers, consider this indictment:

> I would say that a "dull preacher" is a contradiction in terms; if he is dull he is not a preacher. He may stand in a pulpit and talk, but he is certainly not a preacher. With the grand theme and message of the Bible dullness is impossible. This is the most interesting, the most thrilling, the most absorbing subject in the universe; and the idea that this can be presented in a dull manner makes me seriously doubt whether the men who are guilty of this dullness have ever really understood the doctrine they claim to believe, and which they advocate. We often betray ourselves by our manner.[9]

God forbid that we would ever declare His Word in a lifeless, listless manner!

What Happened to the Passion?

Why are so many pulpits without passion? How has the church come to inherit a company of preachers so unlike the early heralds who turned the world upside down with their preaching? There is no one cause for our dullness in the pulpit. Among the factors that have taken the passion out of our pulpits are the following:

Causes of Loss of Passion

► Imitation of seminary lecturers
► Intellectualism
► Inexperience in life
► Inhibited personality
► Ignorance of one's audience

Imitation of seminary lecturers. We unwarily imitate our seminary professors who—for the most part—are not gifted pulpiteers. These learned men are masters of their disciplines (the languages, theology, archaeology, and so on). They are the ones who drill us in the fine aspects of the text but who otherwise do not occupy a rigorous preaching schedule.

In a closed, disciplined environment, content matters more than delivery, and some instructors pride themselves as being more deep than communicative. The nature of seminary allows for this, and the student is highly motivated to grasp the information by grades, graduation, and the cost of education. However, many of us never change this approach after leaving seminary. We take the classroom format into the pulpit and expect the person in the pew to be as motivated and as prepared to receive the mass of information we have prepared for them as we were for our seminary classes. Yet, as we have noted, a lecture and a sermon are not the same!

The seminary lecture is by its very nature condensed material in some respect, void of illustration or application. It is the "raw" Word. It is also well arranged in outline form suitable for note-taking as well as organizing the material. In addition, the burden to grasp and recall the information is placed more upon the student than on the lecturer. Moreover, there is homogeneity in the classroom that is not necessarily found in the church setting. The audience in the class shares the same faith, calling, academic ability, and vocabulary!

The church is vastly different. There the burden of communication is placed on the preacher. The audience can range from the friendly to the hostile, from saved to unsaved, from young children to the elderly, from professional to uneducated, from the wealthy to the impoverished, from those who are eager to hear and obey to those who are utterly apathetic. Such a situation calls for a very different style of delivery. Here we need passionate preaching!

Intellectualism. The early preachers were taught in the world, out in the field. Their emphasis was on changed lives, on souls rescued from hell, and on a religious awakening in the soul. We, on the other hand, are trained in academia, where the emphasis is on scholarship, not on sanctification. We are taught to question, to doubt, to argue, to debate, and to address the cerebral part of Christianity. When we transfer to the environment of the local church, many of us do not change such an approach. The real and "felt" needs of the people are never met or dealt with.

Intellectual preaching need not be passionless preaching. The error of "intellectualism" is that it serves to promote one's learning, to wow the audience, and to omit the uninitiated from the deeper truths. What good is truth delivered enigmatically in the language of the Chaldeans? *Truly intellectual preaching makes truth simple.* It communicates deep truths effectively. It has been said that the test of intelligence is the ability to make the sublime intelligible to the earthly. How true! We should look for the "peek-a-boo" look from the children who listen to us. By that I mean when they strain to look at you between the shoulders of adults because you have arrested their attention. Now true intelligence has performed its finest feat!

Inexperience in life. As we shall see later, time and trials can lead to passion. Our graduates from seminary are for the most part young and inexperienced. The Word has not fully filtered through every fiber of their being, so they are unable to feel deeply about the many subjects that are contained in Scripture. Even prayer may be a stranger to them. "Well, how do you like your new pastor?" one church member asked another. "Fine," she responded. "Our new minister is asking things of God that our other minister didn't even know God had!"

As a minister matures, his passion should increase. Have you ever noticed why older preachers command such attention? It is because they have lived the truth!

Inhibited personality. Some men are by nature shy, timid, and inhibited in regard to their feelings. Unfortunately, our intellectual and reclusive seminary environment appeals to this temperament. In addition, our fear of appearing overemotional, manipulative, and nonintellectual makes us want to subdue any manifestation of emotion, excitement, or pathos in our preaching. One's nature has much to do with our style of preaching. No one need despair, however. Just read what John Broadus said more than a century ago, which I believe still holds true today:

> The chief requisite to an energetic style is an energetic nature. There must be vigorous thinking, earnest if not passionate feeling, and the determined purpose to accomplish some object, or the man's style will have not true, exalted energy. It is in this sense emphatically true that an orator is born, not made. Without these qualities one may give valuable instruction; without them one might preach what silly admirers call "beautiful sermons"; but if a man has no force of character, a passionate soul, he will never be really eloquent. There are, however, timid and sensitive men who, when practice has given them confidence and occasion calls out their powers, exhibit far more masterful nature than they have ever imagined themselves to possess.[10]

My own experience bears this out. I am by nature shy and inhibited, and during my early years I possessed a high degree of stage fright. Yet God has allowed me to go beyond this weakness and to develop a degree of passion in my preaching. If there was hope for me, there is hope for other timid souls.

The desire to write this book came both from what God has done for me and from what I have come to understand the church needs in a preacher. I believe that timid men can become passionate preachers if they are willing to take the principles discussed in the following chapters and adapt them to their personalities. It is not my desire to change a man's personality, only to enhance the passionate *nature* of his personality. Everyone is passionate, only some of us have restrained that passion for various reasons.

Ignorance of the audience. We are not passionate because we are not taught to consider the people to whom we preach. Too many preachers are like the postman; they claim to deliver the mail but care little if we read it. Their job is simply to get us the goods. We preach like that. We deliver the content—the truth—without much concern for whether our people are understanding or even listening to us.

A true conversation takes place when one is speaking and another is listening with comprehension. When either of these two ingredients is missing, communication stops. It is the same with preaching. When our audience stops listening, our sermon is over! Again, in our preaching labs I have watched men preach when all around the class the audience has tuned out, reviewing notes for other classes, some making no eye-contact with the preacher throughout the entire sermon. Yet the preacher was so "into his sermon" that he never noticed that everyone got off at the last stop.

Audience awareness is crucial to passionate preaching. We must know our audience both *before* we preach to them and *as* we preach to them. Lack of awareness leads us to preach sermons that no one needs to hear, or to preach them in a way that no one wants to hear.

Passionate Preaching Can Be Learned

The bottom line for all of us is that we can learn to preach with passion even if we are not passionate by nature. In the course of this book, I will take you through various steps that will lead you to be more passionate in your preaching and, thus, more effective. My aim is that you will never be known as a "boring" or "dull" preacher.

How to Preach with Passion

Chapter 1: Preach with Spiritual Power
Chapter 2: Preach with Conviction
Chapter 3: Preach with Compassion
Chapter 4: Preach with Authority
Chapter 5: Preach with Urgency
Chapter 6: Preach with Brokenness
Chapter 7: Preach with the Whole Body
Chapter 8: Preach with Imagination

1

Preach with Spiritual Power

But you shall receive power when the Holy Spirit has come upon you; and you shall be My witnesses both in Jerusalem, and in all Judea and Samaria, and even to the remotest part of the earth.

—Acts 1:8

The secret to passionate preaching is spiritual power. It is God at work in our lives. We speak of "inspiring sermons," which are sermons with *spirit* in them. We speak of "enthusiastic proclamation," a proclamation with *God in it (en theos).*

Ours is a spiritual work! We are not CEOs of some secular organization like Wal-Mart or IBM. We are God's ministers called and authorized to proclaim His holy Word, a Word that God describes as "living and active and sharper than any two-edged sword, and piercing as far as the division of soul and spirit, of both joints and marrow, and able to judge the thoughts and intentions of the heart" (Heb. 4:12). Spiritual work demands spiritual power.

> *"The secret to passionate preaching is spiritual power. Spiritual work demands spiritual power."*

Ours is a spiritual warfare! Our warfare is not "against flesh and blood, but against the rulers, against the powers, against the world forces of this darkness, against the spiritual forces of wickedness in the heavenly places" (Eph. 6:12). Hence, our armor is spiritual and our weapons are spiritual. The rules of our warfare do not parallel Wall Street or Main Street. *They are divine!* God gives them to us. The apostle Paul, a tested warrior for God, says, "For though we walk in the flesh, we do not war according to the flesh, for the weapons of our warfare are not of the flesh, but divinely powerful for the destruction of fortresses" (2 Cor. 10:3–4).

We will not learn to preach powerfully and passionately from the secular gurus of communication. The secret to powerful preaching lies with God, not man. Skill alone does not make a preacher; God makes the preacher. We err greatly if we mistake skill for spiritual power. To rely upon skill and talent and not upon the power that God supplies is a spiritual and ministerial tragedy.

Passion originates in the heart of God processed through the heart of man. Our God is a consuming fire, awesome in power. When He speaks, the earth quakes. If we would shake the hearts of men, we must be channels through which God can address the hearts of men. We must be ready vessels prepared to execute God's will. When we are passionate about God, we will be passionate in our preaching. The requirements for spiritual power are as follows:

Requirements for Spiritual Power

- ▶ Contrition of soul
- ▶ Confession of sin
- ▶ Communion with the Savior
- ▶ Commission by the Spirit
- ▶ Control by the Spirit
- ▶ Consolation by the saints

The fact about preaching with spiritual power is that we know when we do not have it. In fact, it is much easier to recognize its absence than it is to tell someone how to get it. Often, we refuse to admit the absence of God's power in us and, instead, turn to gimmicks to create this power:

- We purchase a new sound system.
- We reform the worship service to create more powerful impressions.
- We introduce new programs to substitute for ineffective preaching.
- We shorten the sermon and devote more time to the "power" performers.
- We seek the "power encounters" of mysticism.
- We try dramatic preaching, yelling more, and moving illustrations.
- We rely upon PowerPoint presentations and visual imagery.

I am not saying that some of these things are unimportant. Some serve a useful purpose in communication. But they are no substitute for the lack of the Holy Spirit's presence and operation in our lives.

Artificial elements do not give life to a dead sermon offered by a preacher devoid of the Spirit.

The book of Acts is really a demonstration of the power of God in the preaching and living of the disciples. A brief survey of the church in action leads us to connect its power with the Holy Spirit. Examine these references from the book of Acts:

> But you shall receive power when the Holy Spirit has come upon you. (1:8)

> And they were all filled with the Holy Spirit and began to speak with other tongues, as the Spirit was giving them utterance. (2:4)

> Then Peter, filled with the Holy Spirit, said to them. . . . (4:8)

> . . . and they were all filled with the Holy Spirit, and began to speak the word of God with boldness. (4:31)

> But being full of the Holy Spirit, he [Stephen] gazed intently into heaven and saw the glory of God. (7:55)

> But Saul, who was also known as Paul, filled with the Holy Spirit, fixed his gaze upon him, and said . . . (13:9–10)

> And the disciples were continually filled with joy and with the Holy Spirit. (13:52)

These were Christians who were in tune with God and had a deep, personal reliance on the Holy Spirit. We can learn much from them for our living and preaching. Let us consider what it takes to preach with spiritual power.

Contrition of Soul

Preaching in the modern pulpit can be a vainglorious, self-serving act. Only musicians and actors are more apt to surpass us. But preachers are a close third, or perhaps on par. If you doubt me, think of how you responded to the last round of criticism concerning your preaching. Our egos can lead us to a certain self-dependence and delusion.

Spiritual power comes when we realize our utter unworthiness to preach and our total dependence on God *for everything*. God despises a proud heart and opposes the proud. Instead, He chooses to honor those who honor Him (1 Sam. 2:30). We experience our driest and deepest valleys when we rely upon our own strength.

We should look to the prophet Isaiah to seek a similar vision of the exalted and holy God. Isaiah saw

> the Lord sitting on a throne, lofty and exalted, with the train of His robe filling the temple. Seraphim stood above Him, each having six wings; with two he covered his face, and with two he covered his feet, and with two he flew. And one called out to another and said, "Holy, Holy, Holy, is the LORD of hosts, the whole earth is full of His glory." And the foundations of the thresholds trembled at the voice of him who called out, while the temple was filling with smoke. Then I said, "Woe is me, for I am ruined! Because I am a man of unclean lips, and I live among a people of unclean lips; for my eyes have seen the King, the LORD of hosts." Then one of the seraphim flew to me, with a burning coal in his hand which he had taken from the altar with tongs. And he touched my mouth with it and said, "Behold, this has touched your lips; and your iniquity is taken away, and your sin is forgiven."
>
> —Isaiah 6:1–7

Here is a picture of a broken preacher, a man who understood his utter sinfulness and unworthiness to ascend the sacred desk. He will not speak—he dares not speak—until God has touched his lips with a burning coal from the celestial altar.

A story is told of a young preacher who proudly went up to preach and soon after made a mess of his delivery. In great humiliation he descended the platform. A venerable saint said to him, "If you had ascended as you descended, God would have helped you preach with success!"

We must take care of how we ascend to the pulpit if we desire God's power in our preaching. As the Holy of Holies was not available to all—unless they were qualified and entered in purity and reverence—so should it be with the pulpit. We dare not assume the role, treat it as profane, and expect God to bless. He will not! The psalmist in Psalm 24:3–6 lays down the qualifications needed for an ascent to the holy hill of the Lord:

- clean hands;
- a pure heart;
- a true soul; and
- a straight tongue.

Psalm 15 states the same requirements. Here the psalmist qualifies the one who may "abide in God's tent" and who may "dwell on His holy hill" as one who

- walks with integrity and works righteousness,
- speaks truth in his heart,
- does not slander with his tongue,
- does no evil to his neighbor,
- does not take up a reproach against his friend,
- despises a reprobate, and
- honors those who fear the Lord.

Are we such men? Do we yearn to be the man of God spoken of in 1 Timothy 6:11 who flees sin and pursues "righteousness, godliness, faith, love, perseverance, and gentleness"? Our approach to the task of preaching should be with great contrition, humility, and brokenness of heart. The great Reformer, Martin Luther, prayed,

O Lord God, dear Father in heaven, I am indeed unworthy of the office and ministry in which I am to make Thy glory and to nurture and to serve this congregation. But since Thou has appointed me to be a pastor and teacher, and Thy people are in need of the teaching and of the instruction, O be Thou my helper and let Thy holy angels attend me. Then if Thou are pleased to accomplish anything through me, to Thy glory and not to mine or to the praise of men, grant me, out of Thy pure grace and mercy, a right understanding of Thy Word and that I may also diligently perform it. O Lord Jesus Christ, Son of the Living God, Thou Shepherd and Bishop of our soul, send Thy Holy Spirit that He may work with me, yea, that He may work in me to will and to do through Thy divine strength according to Thy good pleasure. Amen.[1]

Here is a man who knew contrition of soul.

Confession of Sin

Sin will keep us from God's power. Yet we always hear of the Bakkers and the Swaggerts of the modern pulpits, luminaries in their oratory but fallen because of their sin. These are warnings to all of us. You dare not rely upon means and methods and tolerate sin in your soul. You dare not preach like the Seraphim and live like Satan!

The key to spiritual power is to keep short accounts of sin with God. We must be often in our confessional closets, expiating our own sins through our own personal Savior, Jesus Christ. God does not favor an unclean preacher. The apostle Peter writes, "For the eyes of the LORD are upon the righteous, and His ears attend to their prayer, but the face of the LORD is against those who do evil" (1 Peter 3:12). Just before this, Peter admonishes husbands to maintain a godly lifestyle with their wives so that their prayers "may not be hindered" (3:7).

> *"The key to spiritual power is to keep short accounts with God."*

The pulpit can be a great help in keeping us from habitual sin if we acknowledge its sanctity and the need for personal holiness as a requirement for our entrance into it to declare God's Word. If we vow not to preach except when we can "lift up holy hands," we will be guaranteed God's help in our ministry. Early in my ministry, I promised that I would never preach if my wife and I were at odds. I've kept that vow through God's grace (though I have had one or two close calls!).

Men of God sin, and men of God must confess their sins. Consider the prayer of Nehemiah (cf. Neh. 1:4–11). Here was a man of God who knew the importance of confessing sin. The same could be said of the prophet Daniel in Daniel chapter 9. And what preacher can forget the penitential prayer of that fallen comrade, David, when he poured out his soul before his God in Psalm 51? He made his confession and cleansing a condition for restored ministry: "Then I will teach transgressors Thy ways, and sinners will be converted to Thee" (Ps. 51:13).

Let me add that the pulpit is no place for the confession of our personal sins to God. We should do that in our study or in our closets. Such show of hypocrisy—that we would use the sacred desk as a pretense for humility and holiness—must be sorrowfully loathsome to God. We must be personally well acquainted with the cross of Christ—the fount of cleansing is for us first. Alexander Maclaren has rightly written, "It takes a crucified man to preach a crucified Savior."[2]

Communion with God

Holiness must also be maintained through a constant and living communion with God. If we are to be leaders of worship, then we must be true worshipers as well. If we are to speak for God, then we must be those who speak *with* God. If we are to lead souls to heaven, then we must be those who descend from heaven with God's Shekinah around us.

Here is where so many of us fail. We do not practice what we preach. Yet we wonder why the power has departed from our preaching. The answer: we have departed from the source of our power, God Himself. Hear the testimony of saintly George Müller: "I saw more clearly than ever that the first and great and primary business to which I ought to attend every day was to have my soul happy in the Lord. The first thing to be concerned about was not how much I might serve the Lord, . . . but how I might get my soul into a happy state, and how my inner [life] might be nourished."[3]

Hence, we need to prioritize our life. God must be first, even before ministry! Warren Wiersbe says, "The most important part of a preacher's life is the part that only God sees—the time alone with God, when you're not sermonizing, when you're not preparing for public ministry, when you are a sinner worshipping a holy God. . . . So I would say to every preacher: Cultivate your spiritual roots and start each day with the Lord."[4]

"Pay close attention to yourself," Paul told Timothy (1 Tim. 4:16). To the Ephesian elders he said, "Be on guard for yourselves" (Acts 20:28). Richard Baxter, in his exposition of Acts 20:28, gives us unforgettable exhortations to communion with God as a must for every preacher. Consider these darts:

> Content not yourselves with being in a state of grace, but be also careful that your graces are kept in vigorous and lively exercise, and that you preach to yourselves the sermons which you study, before you preach them to others. . . .
>
> When your minds are in a holy, heavenly frame, your people are likely to partake of the fruits of it. Your prayers, and praises, and doctrine will be sweet and heavenly to them. They will likely feel when you have been much with God: that which is most on your hearts, is likely to be most in their ears. . . .
>
> Therefore, go then specially to God for life: read some rousing, awakening book, or meditate on the weight of the subject of which you are to speak, and on the great necessity of your people's souls, that you may go in the zeal of the Lord into his house. Maintain, in this manner, the life of grace in yourselves, that it may appear in all your sermons from the pulpit,—that every one who comes cold to the assembly, may have some warmth imparted to him before he departs.[5]

Keys to Communion with God

▶ Read the Scriptures.
▶ Meditate on the Word of God.
▶ Pray consistently.
▶ Grow in love for the Savior.
▶ Worship privately and corporately.
▶ Fast and exercise humility.

Most of us know the keys to communion with God. After all, we are constantly reminding our people to be faithful in them. But all too often we are like that proverbial plumber, fixing everyone else's plumbing except his own. Everyone else's house is high and dry while we drown in our own negligence. May I remind us all of the following:

1. *Develop a personal discipline of reading God's Word, not so much for the formation of a sermon, but for the personal joy of knowing God and His workings in the world.* "I would say," asserts Lloyd-Jones, "that all preachers should read through the whole Bible in its entirety at least once every year."[6]

2. *Let the study of the Word be an exercise in feeding the soul, and not in "fattening up a sermon" for others.* If the sermon feeds you, it will feed others.

3. *Allow enough time in your day for the meditation of what you read and studied.* Take a long walk or ride in the countryside. Find a quiet spot to reflect and ponder the truths encountered in the study. Seek to understand and apply the truth to your heart.

4. *Be in constant prayer.* Prayer should permeate your life. Pray privately. Pray with your spouse and family. Pray with others. Pray especially for all of the ministerial needs such as holiness, boldness, wisdom, open doors, and the right words. Pray for others. Above all, pray "without ceasing" (1 Thess. 5:17) and pray "in the Holy Spirit" (Jude 20).

   Consider the following exhortations to prayer.

   Charles Bridges: "It is prayer alone, then, that gives the

whole strength and efficacy to our different administrations: and that man ceases, if I may use the expression, to be a public Minister from the time he ceases to pray."[7]

Charles Spurgeon: "Prayer may not make you eloquent after the human mode, but it will make you truly so, for you will speak out of the heart; and is not that the meaning of the word eloquence? It will bring fire from heaven upon your sacrifice, and thus prove it to be accepted by the Lord."[8]

5. *Stay in love with your Savior.* Do not forget the day of your salvation. Remember that you were a child of God *before* you became a minister of God, and that you will be a child of God long after you cease to be a minister of God! Your standing with God is based upon neither the size of your church nor the effect of your preaching but upon your adoption in Christ, whereby you cry, "Abba! Father!" (Rom. 8:15). Hence, grow in your love for the Savior.

6. *Make the most of public worship.* Do not be a spectator but a participant. The main goal of the worship service is the worship of God, not the giving or the hearing of your sermon. God, not you, is the main attraction. Let the songs, special music, offerings, and fellowship of God's people provoke you to true worship.

7. *Take special opportunities to devote yourself to protracted times of prayer, fasting, and personal introspection.* Time spent in these spiritual disciplines will show profit in the maintenance of a lively spiritual life.

Robert M. McCheyne has rightly said, "In great measure, according to the purity and perfections of the instruments, will be the success. It is not great talent which God blesses so much as great likeness to Jesus. A holy minister is an awesome weapon in the hand of God."

Commission of the Spirit

Spiritual power comes when we understand that our ministries are not from men but from God. The preacher in some way needs to sense that God has called him to this sacred task. He can do no other. This call needs not only to be felt personally, but it must be affirmed by the church.

The call of the Holy Spirit to the ministry of preaching is open to discussion. Some would place us all on the same level, asserting the priesthood of all believers as sufficient proof that no particular class of individuals has a distinct call from God. Yet we cannot but sense that there are occasions when God does "set apart" men for specific ministry (Acts 13:2: "And while they were ministering to the Lord and fasting, the Holy Spirit said, 'Set apart for Me Barnabas and Saul for the work to which I have called them'"). There is indeed an office of pastor or elder with specific qualifications (cf. 1 Tim. 3:1ff.; Titus 5:17–20; Heb. 13:7, 17).

Throughout the ages, the church has looked for and recognized those whom God has chosen and called for this special task. The power in the pulpit rises or falls upon the recognition—by the preacher and the people alike—that God calls a man to preach. A preacher who doubts his calling will have sufficient reason to doubt his message, and a people who do not recognize that such a man has been sent from God will hesitate to hear and obey.

You are doomed to failure if you are not sure of God's calling. Consider what Charles Bridges has said in regard to the call of the preacher:

> We may sometimes trace Ministerial failure to the very threshold of the entrance into the work. Was the call to the sacred office clear in the order of the church, and according to the will of God? This question bears with vast importance upon the subject. Where the call is manifest, the promise is assured. But if we run unsent, our labours must prove unblest. Many, we fear, have never exercised their minds upon this inquiry. But do not we see the standing ordinance of the church written upon their unfruitful Ministrations—"I sent them not, nor commanded them; *therefore they shall not profit this people at all, saith the Lord*"? (Jer. 23:32).[9]

Spurgeon concurs:

> That hundreds have missed their way and stumbled against a pulpit is sorrowfully evidence from the fruitless ministries and decaying churches which surround us. . . . All are not called to labor in word and doctrine, or to be elders, or to exercise the office of a bishop; nor should all aspire to all; but those should addict themselves to such important engagements who feel, like the apostle, that they have "received this ministry" (2 Cor. 4:1).[10]

"The call comes from God and not from man," says the famous expositor, W. H. Griffith-Thomas. "It must be in some way the immediate appeal of God to the soul: 'Son, go work today in My vineyard.' This call will not be primarily through the Church or a particular denomination, but is the internal work of the Holy Spirit. And as such it will be an 'effectual call'; such a man will inevitably reach the ministry."[11]

D. Martyn-Lloyd Jones asserts,

> A preacher is not a Christian who decides to preach, he does not just decide to do it; he does not even decide to take up preaching as a calling.[12]

> The man who is called by God is a man who realizes what he is called to do, and he so realizes the awfulness of the task that he shrinks from it. Nothing but this overwhelming sense of being called, and of compulsion, should ever lead anyone to preach.[13]

Dr. John F. MacArthur cautions all by saying,

> The pastorate is a calling to men who have a passionate desire to minister. I never compel anyone to go into the ministry. A man must sense the calling of God as a consuming desire in his heart. He is not fit for ministry if he has not sensed the call or if sin in his life is muffling that call.[14]

This commission by God is an indispensable ingredient in a preacher's passion in declaring the Word of the Lord. If you doubt that He sent you, you will be unnerved by both the magnitude of the task and by the response of the audience. Only those commissioned can declare boldly and passionately, "Thus saith the Lord!"

The call of God must also be recognized by the church. When God calls a man, He also informs the church (cf. Acts 6:1–6; 13:1–3). The value of ecclesiastical ordination is that it serves to confirm the call! Pity the poor, insolent preacher who despises the rite of ordination. The approval of the church is not the ultimate proof of the call, but it serves to give the green light to public ministry. With God's calling and the church's backing, we can act as ambassadors of the King and plead with people to be reconciled to God.

Do you want to preach with passion? Has God called you to preach? Then obey the call and go out in the confidence that God supplies. Has the church ordained you to preach? Then speak with ecclesiastical authority. I am a timid soul by nature, but my boldness comes from these twin supports: *the call of God* and *the confirmation of the church*. I can declare God's Word with full assurance, without reservation, and with the understanding that God will bless my ministry.

Controlled by the Spirit

Passion also comes from spiritual power that originates from the Holy Spirit's immediate and personal control of our lives. Much has been said about "anointed preaching," which is that preaching that comes when the preacher is fully controlled by the Holy Spirit. To others, "anointed preaching"—or what is often called "unction"—is a supernatural endowment of power by the Holy Spirit. Lloyd-Jones says,

> I often say that the most romantic place on earth is the pulpit. I ascend the pulpit stairs Sunday after Sunday: I never know what will happen. I confess that sometimes, for various reasons, I come expecting nothing; but suddenly, the power is given. At other times, I think I have a great deal because of

my preparation; but, alas, I find there is no power in it. Thank
God it is like that. I do my utmost, but He controls the supply
and the power; He infuses it.[15]

Tony Sargent studied Lloyd-Jones' preaching and concluded that he
had that sacred anointing. In a book titled *The Sacred Anointing*,
Sargent draws the following analysis about "unction":

- *Unction* is dependent on a "given" element.
- *Unction* is not impeded by the weakness of the preacher.
- The need for *unction* confirms that there is more to preaching
  than speaking.
- In the grace of God, *unction* may still flow when the prepara-
  tion is hurried and inadequate.
- *Unction* causes the preacher to "burn".
- Even the most experienced and godly preachers will still need
  further installments of *unction* for their specific tasks.
- *Unction* involves the congregation.[16]

Sargent then concludes that "unction is what propels the preacher
along. It makes the art of preaching special. This is not to say that
unction is not given in the course of sermon preparation. An anointing can come as the preacher's mind and heart are enlived and warmed
when in the study."[17]

For the average preacher seeking to preach with spiritual power, such
discussion of "anointing" leaves us more miserable than when we first
began. We are led to believe by this description of "anointing" that some
special power is available to the preacher, some supernatural endowment that we must expect, seek, and receive, and that is, in the end, a
capricious endowment by the Holy Spirit upon whom and when He
wills. This is to lay a sore burden upon any poor preacher.

The discussions on anointing do not satisfy me. First, the definitions
of anointing are both nebulous and confusing. Stephen Olford, in his
magnum opus, *Anointed Expository Preaching*, says, "As the filling
suggests an *inward* working of the Spirit, the anointing stresses the
outward clothing with power."[18] A delightful definition, but his subse-

quent explanation is deficient, since it deals with the special anointing of Christ, who all of us preachers know is made from a different cloth!

Consider Sangster's enigmatic explanation of unction:

> Unction is that mystic plus in preaching which no one else can define and no one (with any spiritual sensitivity at all) can mistake. Men have it, or they do not have it. It is a thing apart from good sermon outlines, helpful spiritual insights, wise understanding, or eloquent speech. It can use all these media—and dispense with them. It is rare, undefinable, and unspeakably precious.[19]

Thanks a lot! "Unspeakably precious" but "undefinable and rare"? *It is my conclusion that such a thing does not exist.* We should be relieved of this unspeakable burden placed upon us by those who teach this about preaching. Every example given of men who preached with unction were men endowed with manifold speaking and intellectual abilities. Where are the men with no talent or abilities? If unction is all of God, surely we would see the plain, ignorant, untalented yet godly preacher so endowed! Even uneducated Moody was a naturally eloquent speaker!

Biblical anointing had to do with ordination to a task (cf. Exod. 28:41), a consecration (cf. Exod. 29:36; 40:13), a designation to office (cf. Judg. 9:8; 1 Sam. 9:16), and a rubbing of ointment or perfume upon the body (cf. Luke 7:46; Rev. 3:9). There is no question that Christ had a special anointing (Luke 4:18; Acts 10:38), and that the Holy Spirit is that anointing given to all (cf. 1 John 2:20, 27).

That the apostolic church preached with spiritual power is everywhere obvious. The power came from the following sources:

1. *The promise of the Holy Spirit* (Acts 1:8). We see the demonstration of power in the preaching on the day of Pentecost (Acts 2:1ff.).
2. *The personal relationship with the risen Savior* (Acts 4:13–20). The apostles experienced a living faith; they knew beyond all doubt that Christ was their risen Lord.

3. *The prayer for special boldness to preach* (Acts 4:29–31). The power came in response to prayer.
4. *The powerful control of the Holy Spirit* (Acts 4:8; 13:9, 52; cf. 6:3, 5).

We can expect to be used by the Holy Spirit in preaching when we are under His constant control (not just in the pulpit; cf. Eph. 5:18), when we do not grieve or quench the Spirit (Eph. 4:30; 1 Thess. 5:19), and when we do not resist Him (Acts 7:51). Every preacher can experience God's power if he simply yields his life to the obedience of Christ and seeks faithfully to carry out His charge! An obedient preacher should expect God to bless the Word preached (Isa. 55:11). As saintly McCheyne said, "A holy minister is an awesome weapon in the hands of God."

Powerful preaching, therefore, is neither measured by the size of the church nor by the charisma and eloquence of the preacher. It is rather the impact of the Word uttered by the preacher upon the hearer. You may be a powerful preacher even though your congregation may be small! Congregation size is not a just criterion to determine if a preacher is preaching with spiritual power. The size of a congregation involves many variables, many of which are not translatable or reproducible to other congregations. Yet spiritual power is available to every preacher who wishes to become an instrument of God for good, a clean channel for God's Word to be poured out upon the hearts of His people.

> *"Every preacher can experience God's power if he simply yields his life in obedience to Christ and seeks faithfully to carry out His charge."*

The Consolation of the Saints

Powerful preaching comes as a result of God's people interacting with us in our preaching. We dare not minimize the importance of the congregation upon our preaching. How do they increase and improve this "preaching with spiritual power"?

First, by their *intercessions*. We definitely need the prayers of our people. The apostle Paul knew the importance of prayer on his behalf. Consider how often he asked for prayer in regard to his preaching:

> *And pray on my behalf, that utterance may be given to me in the opening of my mouth, to make known with boldness the mystery of the gospel, for which I am an ambassador in chains; that in proclaiming it I may speak boldly, as I ought to speak.*
>
> —Ephesians 6:19–20

> *. . . praying at the same time for us as well, that God may open up to us a door for the word, so that we may speak forth the mystery of Christ, for which I have also been imprisoned; that I may make it clear in the way I ought to speak.*
>
> —Colossians 4:3–4

> *Finally, brethren, pray for us that the word of the Lord may spread rapidly and be glorified, just as it did also with you.*
>
> —2 Thessalonians 3:1

If such a powerful preacher as the apostle Paul relied upon the intercessions of the saints, what about the rest of us who do not hold a candle to the apostle! We should enlist our people to pray specifically for the proclamation of the Word on the Lord's Day. The "furnace" of Charles H. Spurgeon is legendary. He had his people pray as he preached. One biographer describes the pastor's prayer meeting held by Spurgeon on Thursday evening. "This was an extra gathering, specially convened for the purpose of pleading for a blessing upon the Word he was about to preach; and most refreshing and helpful it always proved both to himself and to the people."[20] For anyone wishing to have power like Spurgeon, he should also have the people pray for his preaching.

The people of God can also improve our preaching by *their interaction with us.* Our people make us powerful preachers. They are unfortunately our "guinea pigs," for we practice on them. Here is where a patient, wise audience is of help to us. They provide a forum for us to develop our trade and to hone our preaching skills. I heard a church leader say that small churches produce great preachers and pastors for they know the value of allowing the men to grow in their skills as they minister—sometimes fumbling—to them. Even Spurgeon remarked that he used the weekday meeting as an opportunity to develop his extemporaneous style of preaching.

God's people can also be an invaluable resource in providing *constructive criticism* to our preaching. If we are wise and humble, we will welcome these constructive suggestions to our preaching, even though they may come in a tactless fashion. Our insecurities and pride may prevent this from happening. We may quickly stifle any help we might receive from our people. Then we will never develop into better preachers and we will cement bad habits or an ineffective style or spirit. Bad habits are tough to break. Consider how even the powerful preacher Apollos was helped by some laymen in his sermon content and delivery (cf. Acts 18:26–28). God will send us our "Aquilas and Priscillas" to take us aside and explain to us not only that we missed the point of the text but also that we just are not relating to people. Consider yourself a novice until the saints give you their approval.

A Sober Reminder

I close this chapter with Paul's reminder that a close walk with God is the key to usefulness:

> *Now in a large house there are not only gold and silver vessels, but also vessels of wood and of earthenware, and some to honor and some to dishonor. Therefore, if any man cleanses himself from these things, he will be a vessel for honor, sanctified, useful to the Master, prepared for every good work*
> —2 Timothy 2:20–21

Resolve to be that sanctified vessel!

2

Preach with Conviction

. . . for we cannot stop speaking what we have seen and heard.
—Acts 4:20

I recently came across this curious thought:

A preacher was approached by some members of his congregation about trouble in the church. Airing their grievances, they made all sorts of charges against those with whom they were at odds. Responding to their complaints, the preacher said, "You're right. You're absolutely right." The next night, however, another group came to his home and told their side of the story. He listened very quietly, and when they had finished, said, "You're right. You're absolutely right." His wife, working in the kitchen, overheard everything. As soon as the parishioners left, she rushed into the living room and exclaimed, "You're just about the most wishy-washy individual I've every seen!" To that he responded, "You're right. You're absolutely right!"[1]

All too often men in the pulpit seem to resemble this character, wishy-washy preachers who stand for nothing, who lull their hearers into complacency, who drone their audiences into a Christless eternity. A preacher of the gospel by definition is a man who stands for something, who preaches with strong personal convictions about the matters at hand. Such a man cannot but be passionate in his preaching.

Passionate preaching almost always comes from a man who holds the truth he proclaims with deep personal convictions. They are the truths for which he would die. Men hold opinions, but convictions hold the man. Convictions are spiritual instincts that drive us to action regardless of the circumstances. Yet convictions about the truths we preach is what is sadly lacking in our pulpits today. We have too many wishy-washy, half-in, half-out, boneless, spineless preachers in our pulpits today, and a wishy-washy pulpit produces wishy-washy people.

> con✦vic✦tion *n*. the state of being convinced; firm belief; convincing, as of a truth.[2]

The Bible is replete with examples of men and women who stood for what they believed, who were willing to suffer unspeakable harm for their convictions, and who were even willing to die for what they believed was right. I hold them up as role models for us. Consider the passionate convictions of the following servants of God:

- *The conviction of Joshua:* "Choose for yourselves today whom you will serve . . . but as for me and my house, we will serve the LORD" (Josh. 24:15).
- *The conviction of restored Samson:* "Let me die with the Philistines!" (Judg. 16:30).
- *The conviction of Ruth:* "Thus may the LORD do to me, and worse, if anything but death parts you and me" (Ruth 1:17).
- *The conviction of Samuel:* "Has the LORD as much delight in burnt offerings and sacrifices as in obeying the voice of the LORD? . . . Because you have rejected the word of the LORD, He has also rejected you from being king" (1 Sam. 15:22–23).
- *The conviction of Nathan the prophet:* "You are the man!" (2 Sam. 12:7).
- *The conviction of Elijah:* "How long will you hesitate between two opinions? If the LORD is God, follow Him; but if Baal, follow him" (1 Kings 18:21).
- *The conviction of Esther:* ". . . and if I perish, I perish" (Esther 4:16).
- *The conviction of Job:* "Shall we indeed accept good from God and not accept adversity?" (Job 2:10).
- *The conviction of Daniel:* "Daniel made up his mind that he would not defile himself" (Dan. 1:8).
- *The conviction of Shadrach, Meshach, and Abed-nego:* "But even if He does not, let it be known to you, O king, that we are not going to serve your gods or worship the golden image that you have set up" (Dan. 3:18).
- *The conviction of John the Baptist:* "You brood of vipers, who warned you to flee from the wrath to come?" (Matt. 3:7) and, "It is not lawful for you to have her" (14:4).
- *The conviction of the apostles:* "Whether it is right in the sight

of God to give heed to you rather than to God, you be the judge; for we cannot stop speaking what we have seen and heard" (Acts 4:19–20) and, "We must obey God rather than men" (5:29).

- *The conviction of Stephen:* "You men who are stiff-necked and uncircumcised in heart and ears are always resisting the Holy Spirit; you are doing just what your fathers did" (Acts 7:51).
- *The conviction of Paul:* "For to me, to live is Christ, and to die is gain" (Phil. 1:21).
- *The conviction of John:* "I . . . was on the island called Patmos, because of the word of God and the testimony of Jesus" (Rev. 1:9).
- *The conviction of our Lord and Savior:* "The Son of Man must suffer many things, and be rejected by the elders and chief priests and scribes, and be killed, and be raised up on the third day" (Luke 9:22).

The list of God's saints who lived and preached with conviction can go on indefinitely, from the Reformer Martin Luther, who made his historic stand at Worms, to Eric Liddell, the Scottish runner who distinguished himself by refusing to race on the Lord's Day during the Olympics.

Men who have convictions and live by them will also preach with conviction. Still, a gap does exist in some preachers between preaching God's Word and preaching passionately. We preach His Word, but not passionately. We preach truth, but not with verve or fire burning deep in our bones. Much has to do with what we preach, and not so much in what we truly believe. As preachers convinced of the Bible as the Word of God and committed to preach that Word, we should never lack passion. The Word of God alone is a fountain of inspiration (Pss. 19:7–13; 119:1ff.); it is powerful (Heb. 4:12–13), sufficient (2 Tim. 3:16–17), and divinely effective (Isa. 55:11).

Preaching with conviction rests on these simple premises:

Principles for Preaching with Conviction

- ▶ Major on the major themes.
- ▶ Preach the main thesis of the text.

- ▶ Preach the jugular text.
- ▶ Preach the orthodox doctrines.
- ▶ Minor on the minor themes.
- ▶ Meditate on the text to be preached.

The expository preacher may be at a great disadvantage when it comes to preaching with passion. Since he has chosen a style of preaching that elects to go chapter-by-chapter, verse-by-verse through the entire books of the Bible, he also must preach through books or portions of books that may not deeply excite his heart, or the hearts of his hearers. Cognitive, sequential preaching is not always passionate or exciting.

May I suggest that even expository preachers may preach with deep personal convictions if they but follow a few guidelines on preaching?

Major on Major Bible Themes

The great preachers are those who preach the great themes of Scripture. Topical and textual preachers have the advantage over expository preachers because they can pick and choose those themes that excite their hearts and upon which they feel deeply. The expositor, however, must preach the next section regardless of whether it excites him. *The style dictates the content!* The scriptural landscape is not all adorned with easily applicable, readily available, and lofty truths. Some sections call for great exegetical skill to mine out the ore and great homiletical skill to deliver a stirring, relevant message.

So what can the expositor do? First, he can be wise in the selection of the book that he plans to exposit. Since the Bible is an encyclopedia of books and themes, he has a choice in selecting the book of the Bible that will be most important to the people. For the church, the New Testament books take precedent over the Old Testament. For church planters, I recommend an exposition of Matthew, then Acts, followed by Romans and 1 Corinthians. Almost every chapter in these four books will be extremely vital for the establishment and maturing of the church.

The Old Testament makes for great expository preaching, and obviously some books are more foundational for the church than others (e.g., Genesis vs. Leviticus). Some Old Testament books appear to be timeless (e.g., Psalms, Proverbs), whereas others need a great deal of bridge-building to make them palatable to our audience (e.g., the Minor Prophets).

I in no way want to minimize the inspiration of all Scripture nor do I seek to promote neglect of the preaching of the whole counsel of God. I simply want to reveal the obvious for expositors. If you had a choice between Romans and 2 Chronicles to exposit on Sunday mornings, which would excite your heart? Which would contain the major themes your people urgently need to learn and assimilate into their lives? The answer is obvious. Hence, we would be wise to select our books carefully.

Preach the Main Thesis of the Text

By preaching the main thesis of the text I mean that as expositors we must preach the subject and predicate of the paragraph and chapter. Some expositors think that they must explain every jot and tittle, every grammatical and syntactical nuance, or every stylistic tangent in order to be truly called an "expositor." Honestly, not many of us can be really passionate about a Greek particle! I doubt if our people have the same enthusiasm for tenses and moods of verbs.

Exposition is much like serving chicken for dinner. We have killed the chicken, plucked its feathers, and dismembered its body, but you will never see chicken feet or necks served on the platter. You serve the best part of the chicken. (As a boy, I recall being the recipient of the neck! It had to do for want of meat, but I would have preferred to have the drumstick!)

Why do we serve our people less than the main thesis of the text? Why do we hesitate to lay before them the grand themes unfolded by the Gospel writers and instead demand that they swoon under the descriptions and explanations of lesser themes, of peripheral matters. If we would identify the main thesis of the text, see its vitality to the original recipients, to us, and to our audience, we would soon feel deeply about it and would preach it with vitality. A sermon is not an exercise in exegesis, but a declaration of a truth to move us to moral action. It is truth mediated through a man. Anything less than this can be accomplished without the preacher.

> *"A sermon is not an exercise in exegesis, but a declaration of a truth to move us to moral action."*

Preach the Jugular Text

The jugular vein is the main vein, the life-sustaining artery in our body. To strike the jugular vein is to deliver a mortal blow. The same applies to preaching the Scriptures. If you are a textual or topical preacher, then select the jugular texts, those texts that contain the whole of the doctrine in one or two verses.

Preaching the jugular text is like serving filet mignon for every meal. The preacher simply searches the Scriptures for the texts that speak on the major themes of the Bible. For a sermon on origins, you go to Genesis 1; for a sermon on sin, Genesis 3; for holiness, Isaiah 6; for confession of sin, Psalm 51; for the new birth, John 3; and so on!

Herein lies the secret to revivalist and itinerate preachers: they simply choose the texts that contain the truth that excites their hearts, and then they deliver this truth with passion. We can learn much from them.

A word of caution is in order here. A text should not become a pretext. A thorough exegesis must precede our sermon, even if we expound no more than a single verse. The verse should be studied thoroughly within its grammatical, historical, and literary context. No preacher should ever preach on a passage that he does not truly and fully understand. It is our job to *declare truth,* not to give out sermons.

Preach the Orthodox Doctrines

Orthodoxy excites! Orthodoxy is the cardinal doctrines of the Christian faith, tenaciously held throughout the centuries and delivered to us by faithful and fearless defenders of the faith. *Orthodox doctrines are worth dying for!* Orthodoxy moved Jude to charge us passionately to "contend earnestly for the faith which was once for all delivered to the saints" (Jude 3). Jude's passion explodes on the pages of the Bible.

We need to be well acquainted with doctrines and theology. The whole point of studying theology in seminary is to make us aware of the cardinal truths contained in Scripture, and to understand how they affect the human race. Unfortunately, theology can be studied solely for academic purposes, and we tend to preach it in much the same way. The dry professor of theology produces a dry preacher of theology. Such need not be the case. Theology, if it be true, *biblical* theology, should make our hearts burn like those of the Emmaus disciples (cf. Luke 24:32).

Every preacher should be a theologian. He should know his doctrine because every sermon is a doctrinal sermon—an unfolding of some divine truth revealed in the Scriptures. If a sermon does not unfold a specific doctrine, if it does not elucidate or explain a tenet of the faith, it is not a biblical sermon. In short, we are failing to "preach the Word." For this reason, we should be well acquainted with our theology. Our theology books should be at arm's length, and we should make ready use of them as we prepare our sermons.

> *"Every preacher should be a theologian. He should know his doctrine because every sermon is a doctrinal sermon—an unfolding of some divine truth revealed in the Scriptures."*

Let me make two observations here in regard to preaching with conviction. First, concentrate on the major orthodox doctrines. Identify them, isolate them, instruct yourself on them, and instill them in your audience. Paul preached the cross, not baptism (1 Cor. 1:17). Notice the wisdom of the apostle in isolating the lofty doctrines. Did baptism matter to Paul? Of course it did! But Paul knew that the gospel is what saves, not baptism. So he preached the cardinal doctrine of the cross. The cross excites me; modes of baptism do not. If we would preach with conviction, then we must identify the orthodox doctrines that matter to us, those that are indispensable, nonnegotiable truths. We must preach these with the white-hot conviction that our people must hold them as dearly as we do.

The second observation is this: preach doctrines in the same way God does! In history, in story, in the context of human life—not in the dry, analytical format of a book on theology. Every doctrine is learned in the context of God's dealing with His people. He reveals Himself in everyday life and circumstances. There is no better way to communicate truth. Go and do likewise.

Minor on the Minor Themes

Not only should we make it our ambition to major on the major Bible themes if we would preach with conviction but also we must wisely abstain from those minor themes that steal the thunder of God's revealed will. The husk is important to the development of the grain, but only the one is edible; therefore, only one is vital. The same can be said about revealed truth. Too much preaching today is preaching based on minor themes:

- historical backgrounds,
- ecclesiastical traditions,
- extrabiblical themes,
- unsettled theological disputes, and
- political controversies.

On occasion, a preacher can get excited about some of these issues—especially political and controversial issues. Some people love a good fight! But a steady diet of politics or controversies does not profit the soul, nor can the preacher sustain his passion in a truly godly manner if he continually preaches minor themes. Perhaps this is what Paul referred to when he spoke of the man who "has a morbid interest in controversial questions and disputes about words, out of which arise envy, strife, abusive language, evil suspicions, and constant friction" (1 Tim. 6:3–5). Or when he charged Timothy to avoid "worldly and empty chatter and the opposing arguments of what is falsely called 'knowledge'" (1 Tim. 6:20); and again to "avoid worldly and empty chatter, for it will lead to further ungodliness" (2 Tim. 2:16). Or his words to Titus when he challenged him to "shun foolish controversies and genealogies and strife and disputes about the Law; for they are unprofitable and worthless" (Titus 3:9).

Sangster says,

> If the sermon titles which are printed on Saturday evenings in some newspapers are anything to go by, many preachers are still toying with trifles. Nor is it a fault of the less able men. One sometimes hears a man with a good deal of homiletical skill weaving something out of nothing in the pulpit and leaving the hungry listener wishing that half that cleverness had been spent on the marrow of the gospel and had dealt in a serious way with the things by which man lives.[3]

Meditate on the Text

For us to preach with conviction, we need to let the truth in the text burn in our hearts until we feel like Jeremiah, when the Word becomes like a burning fire shut up in our bones (Jer. 20:9), or like the apostles who said, "we cannot stop speaking about what we have seen and heard" (Acts 4:20).

What steps do we take to create a fire within us?

1. First, we seek an *exegetical* understanding of the text: *What does it mean?*
2. Second, we seek an experimental understanding of the text: *What does this mean to me?*
3. Third, we seek a homiletical understanding of the text: *What truth do my people need to hear from this text? How can I serve it to them?*

These three steps provide the combustible ingredients to create a blaze in one's soul. Truth discovered warms the mind; truth applied in our lives warms the heart; and the necessity of imparting this same truth to others sets the pulpit aflame.

Passionate preaching cannot bypass any one of these steps. There is no shortcut. Dr. John MacArthur Jr. has emphasized the nature of preaching as "hard work": "We must stay in our seats until the work is done!"[4] We are in too much of a hurry to preach, I fear, and when we do preach it is only an exercise of duty and not of burning conviction.

Conviction about some biblical truth begins with our exegesis, with the tedious spadework of seeking to understand what the Bible means by what it says. The text to be preached must be so thoroughly researched that we could answer any question in relation to it. We must feel that we have understood exactly what the writer intended to say! Every jot and tittle has been dissected, every tributary has been explored, every thought has been exhumed until there is nothing left to discover. *Then* we are ready to proceed to the next step. But it is at this first step that many preachers fail. Laziness fells some of us; distraction fells others. Want of good exegetical tools fells still others. For others, it is to begin too late in the week so that we end up with "Saturday-night specials!" The preacher is primarily an exegete! We must live up to that job description.

The truth discovered must, in turn, be personally applied. Like the proverbial cow, once ingested into the cranial stomach, it must be transferred to the experimental stomach, where it is digested to do us personal, spiritual good. A text that has not benefited us in some way will not be communicated with any sense of excitement or urgency. The text must feed us if it would feed others. Obviously, this experimental application takes time and spiritual readiness. We, too, can become "stiff-necked and uncircumcised in heart and ear" so as to resist the Holy Spirit's ministry to our own good! Remember, *a cold heart makes for cold preaching!*

The final step is to seek a *homiletical* understanding of the text, to look for ways to apply the truth to the hearts of our people. A pastor knows his sheep, knows well the condition of his flock, and knows what truth they need for the hour. He also knows their peculiar humors and habits so that he searches for the best approach at communicating the truth so that it will do them the most good. Our meditation on the text should extend even to the form of delivery we use to communicate the Word of God. We will be convinced not only of the truth but also of the way the truth is served.

Conviction Is Contagious

Preaching with conviction is preaching with passion. I've endeavored to help you get conviction about what you preach, to help you feel deeply about what you are going to say to your people. Allow me to close this chapter with two quotations that spoke to my heart.

> A preacher who feels an interest in his subject will always be listened to. His hearers may not believe his doctrine; they may be captious, critical, fastidious; but they *will hear*. He cannot have an inattentive auditory; the thing is impossible. Few eyes will wander, few minds will be listless, few hearts will be indifferent. Those to whom he preaches may complain; they may hear and hate; but they will hear. No preacher can sustain the attention of a people unless he feels his subject; nor can he long sustain it, unless he feels deeply. If he would make others solemn, he must himself be solemn; he must have fellowship with the truth he utters.[5]

> Let a man be laid hold of by certain truths, let him see them as facts and not only as feelings, let him see them lying at the heart of reality and with immense significance, not only to himself but to the whole race, and they will give an urge and warmth and conviction to his proclamation which is quite transforming.[6]

Preacher, go and preach with conviction!

3

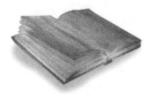

Preach with Compassion

And Jesus was going about all the cities and the villages, teaching in their synagogues, and proclaiming the gospel of the kingdom, and healing every kind of disease and every kind of sickness. And seeing the multitudes, He felt compassion for them, because they were distressed and downcast like sheep without a shepherd.

—Matthew 9:35–36

Preaching is not merely an exercise in speech or oratory. Preaching is not an end in itself. It is a means to an end, and that being the helping of another human being. Preaching is one soul pleading to another, *"Be reconciled to God!"* (2 Cor. 5:20). Some men become preachers because they love the task, the accompanying glory, and the feeling of power. But such will never preach with passion. It is the burden for others that creates passion in our preaching. "Others" becomes our pastoral cry! Lloyd-Jones hits the mark when he writes,

> To love to preach is one thing, to love those to whom we preach is quite another. The trouble with some of us is that we love preaching, but we are not always careful to make sure that we love the people to whom we are actually preaching. If you lack this element of compassion for the people you will also lack the pathos which is a very vital element in all true preaching.[1]

Passionate, powerful preaching is characterized by compassion for people. Compassion is feeling the same as others, carrying their burdens, sharing their pain, weeping when they weep.

> **com♦pas♦sion** *n.* a feeling of deep sympathy and sorrow for someone struck by misfortune, accompanied by a desire to alleviate the suffering; mercy.[2]

Compassion is what characterized the ministry of the Lord Jesus: "seeing the multitudes, He felt compassion for them, because they were distressed and downcast like sheep without a shepherd" (Matt. 9:35–36). The Greek word translated "felt compassion" speaks of the movement of the inward parts (heart, liver, lungs, and so on) in response to the pain and misery observed.[3] The whole person is deeply affected! Christ was no mere preacher; He was a lover of mankind. His whole ministry was an outpouring of His compassion for us.

- Compassion moved the Lord Jesus to associate with sinners (Matt. 9:13) and thus attracted them to Himself (Luke 15:1).
- Compassion moved the Lord Jesus to liberate mankind from the cold legalism of the Pharisees (Matt. 12:7).
- Compassion moved the Lord Jesus to a ministry of healing diseases and infirmities (Matt. 14:14).
- Compassion moved the Lord Jesus to feed the hungry masses (Matt. 15:22).
- Compassion moved the Lord Jesus to restore the sight of the blind beggars in Jericho (Matt. 20:34).
- Compassion moved the Lord Jesus to touch the untouchable leper, healing him (Mark 1:41).
- Compassion moved the Lord Jesus to raise the widow's son from the dead (Luke 7:13).

"It is our burden for others that creates passion in our preaching."

Hence, the words that Christ spoke proceeded from a life deeply affected by those to whom He ministered. He identified with us, suffered with us, and ultimately died for us. *Are we like Christ?* Or are we aloof from the everyday drudgery of mankind? Do we despise the afflicted, loathe the godless, flee the needy, avoid the helpless, fear contamination by the perverse, and shut up our hearts from the pain of identifying with the hurts of others? How dare we then ascend the pulpit to speak words of comfort and encouragement when there is no feeling in our words? Miserable comforters are we! Baxter says,

> Brethren, can you look believingly on your miserable people, and not perceive them calling to you for help? There is not a sinner whose case you should not so far compassionate, as to be willing to relieve them at a much dearer rate than this comes to. Can you see them, as the wounded man by the way, and unmercifully pass by?[4]

Remove the Common Fetishes of Preaching

Our preaching is lifeless because it comes from stony hearts. The fact is that we preach for all the wrong reasons. Our aim is too low. If we were honest with ourselves, we would be embarrassed to admit our real motives in preaching, that it is not to bring spiritual balm to the afflicted of God's flock. No, the motives are often much less noble, more carnal, more selfish, and more mercenary in nature.

Common Fetishes of Preaching

- ▶ Preaching for hire
- ▶ Preaching to draw a crowd
- ▶ Preaching to please the audience
- ▶ Preaching to promote our learning
- ▶ Preaching to print or publish
- ▶ Preaching to protect our "kingdom"
- ▶ Preaching to pass the time

If we are honest with ourselves, we will admit that we have often laid our sacrifices upon the high places mentioned here, and not upon the true, sacred altar of God's purpose for preaching. We preach for the wrong reasons, and then we wonder why we cannot put heart and soul into it. Let me elucidate.

1. *We preach for hire.* Preaching is both a calling and a vocation, but it is foremost a divine calling. We should pay to preach more than we are willing to get paid for preaching. The Word of God warns us against serving for money (cf. 1 Peter 5:2; 2 Tim. 6:5–10). Yet we can easily become "guns for hire," mercenaries in need of a livelihood, and so we preach to make a buck. A bought preacher is a pitiful preacher; his sermons and his life are pitiful. We would do well to imitate Elisha in his ministry rather than to have our ministries infected by the leprosy of covetousness (cf. 2 Kings 5). Better that we make tents to finance the ministry than be a hireling to a people in need of a prophet

to tickle their ears. Paul could be bold and passionate because he "coveted no one's silver or gold or clothes" (Acts 20:33).

2. *We preach to draw a crowd.* America, nay, the world is in love with large crowds, and we are in competition with one another to see who can build the biggest church. The pathway to the high places is lined with preachers sacrificing truth for the pleasure of drawing a crowd. Under the guise of evangelism, of relating to a new generation, and of making the truth relevant, we have sacrificed the truth that saves and sanctifies on the altar of numbers.

3. *We preach to please the audience.* We preach to please people, not to do them spiritual good. We give placebo sermons instead of sound, healthy words that benefit people for the present and for eternity. Such preachers are afraid to utter the hard and necessary truths for fear of losing their audience!

    We must ask ourselves, "Are we here to entertain a crowd or are we called to turn people to Christ and to holy living?" We have already been warned about the mood of some against sound doctrine (cf. 2 Tim. 4:3–4). Christ taught us by His own example that we ought never to play to the crowd (cf. John 6:64–69). Or, as Paul would say, "If I were still trying to please men, I would not be a bond-servant of Christ" (Gal. 1:10). As ministers of God, we are called to declare to people what they *need* to hear, not what they *want* to hear! We should have the attitude of the pastor who was reprimanded by his deacons: "Pastor, you're rubbing the cat the wrong way!" "Well, then," said the pastor, "turn the cat around!" We ought never to be afraid to rub the cat the wrong way.

4. *We preach to promote our learning.* Some of us think that the pulpit is a place to wow the audience with our learning. We think it a triumph when we preach over their heads and no one comprehends, and the service ends with a comment like, "You were sure *deep* today, pastor." Such may be good for our intellectual egos, but it does little for the spiritual needs of our people. Clarity is the axiom! We *must* be understood or all is lost! The great *apostle* Paul had this as his goal (cf. 1 Cor. 14:19).

Our Lord was a preacher of the simple and had great effect upon the masses. Luke wrote that "all the people were hanging upon His words" (Luke 19:48). It is said that John Wesley first preached his sermons to the maids to be sure that even the simplest would understand him.

5. *We preach to print or publish.* It is a reversal of purposes to think that we can use our audience as a means to this end. Everyone knows that the printed word is not like the spoken word. In almost every case where a great preacher has had his sermons printed it is because his sermons did his people much good. If your sermons are worthy of preaching, they may be worthy of printing. But keep to your main priority: *preach to help your people.*

6. *We preach to protect our "kingdoms."* Like the enemies of the gospel in the apostolic days, we may refrain from declaring the whole counsel of God and instead possess the spirit of Diotrophes (3 John 9–10). God's people are no one's possession except His. Our goal is to present everyone complete in Christ (Col. 1:28), not to make them our clones.

7. *We preach to pass the time.* Some men hold to a pulpit as a security blanket until they find greener pastures or until they reach retirement age and qualify for retirement benefits. We may impede the work of God by occupying a post with no desire to advance the cause of Christ. A "lame-duck" minister is just that—*lame!* We should all follow the refrain given by one CEO: "Lead, follow, or get out of the way!"

Why Preach?

We mistake our calling if we think that our task is merely to preach beautiful sermons or to go through the motions of teaching the Bible. Preaching is not an end in itself; it is a means to an end. Preaching is but one of many spiritual means that God has ordained to bring a lost world into harmony with Himself. The goal of ministry is clearly given to us by Paul in his letter to the Colossians: "We proclaim Him, admonishing every man and teaching every man with all wisdom, that

we may present every man complete in Christ. And for this purpose
also I labor, striving according to His power, which mightily works
within me" (1:28–29). "To present every man complete in Christ" is
the goal of the minister, and Paul declares that it deserves to be done
with *total abandonment!*

The same thought is expressed in the Pastoral Epistles:

> *All Scripture is inspired by God and profitable for teaching,
> for reproof, for correction, for training in righteousness; that
> the man of God may be adequate, equipped for every good
> work.*
> —2 Timothy 3:16–17

> *Preach the word; be ready in season and out of season; re-
> prove, rebuke, exhort, with great patience and instruction.*
> —2 Timothy 4:2

> *. . . holding fast the faithful word which is in accordance with
> the teaching, that he may be able both to exhort in sound
> doctrine and to refute those who contradict.*
> —Titus 1:9

The ultimate goal of preaching is "the equipping of the saints for
the work of service, to the building up of the body of Christ" (Eph.
4:12). It is easy for us to forget this. The use of the pulpit and the
worship service for entertainment and theatrical performances can
make us miss this mark. Even among evangelicals there is the subtle
desire to be the "great preacher" or the "great expositor," instead of
the great doer of good to our people.

"The ministry would be a great place," someone has said, "if it were
not for the people." Such a remark misses the whole purpose of ministry. People *are* our business—our only business—and true preaching is to be *people-oriented*. The apostle Paul reminded the Ephesian
elders of their purposes both by a strong exhortation (cf. Acts 20:28)
and by his personal testimony as to how he personally ministered
among them. Catch Paul's compassionate heart in his words:

You yourselves know, from the first day that I set foot in Asia, how I was with you the whole time, serving the Lord with all humility and with tears and with trials which came upon me through the plots of the Jews; how I did not shrink from declaring to you anything that was profitable, and teaching you publicly and from house to house. . . . That night and day for a period of three years I did not cease to admonish each one with tears.

—Acts 20:18–20, 31

When was the last time you wept for your people? When did your tears and weeping arrest your speaking? When were you last so overwhelmed by your love for your congregation that your words went forth mingled with tears? Spurgeon writes of George Whitefield,

> Hear how Whitefield preached, and never dare be lethargic again. Winter says of him that "sometimes he exceedingly wept, and was frequently so overcome, that for a few seconds you would suspect he never would recover; and when he did, nature required some little time to compose himself. I hardly ever knew him go through a sermon without weeping more or less. His voice was often interrupted by his affections."[5]

Every preacher wants to have the ability and acclaim of George Whitefield, but few have his compassion imbedded in his soul, a compassion that permeated every fiber of that tireless, itinerant herald. Whitefield would say,

> You blame me for weeping; but how can I help it, when you will not weep for yourselves, although your own immortal souls are on the verge of destruction, and for aught I know, you are hearing your last sermon, and may never more have an opportunity to have Christ offered to you?[6]

Therein lies the secret to Whitefield's success. It was not his capabilities, but his compassion. His love and concern for people drove the engines of his oratory!

> **"When were you last so overwhelmed
> by your love for your congregation
> that your words went forth mixed
> with tears?"**

Our sermons should help people, and such sermons can only be constructed if we have people upon our hearts as we prepare them! We dare not be like the worthless shepherds of Israel who became the object of prophetic denunciation. They were castigated because they did not have the welfare of God's people as their highest priority (cf. Jer. 23:1–2). Note Ezekiel's record of the Lord's condemnation of such shepherds:

> *Woe, shepherds of Israel who have been feeding themselves!
> Should not the shepherds feed the flock? You eat the fat and
> clothe yourselves with the wool, you slaughter the fat sheep
> without feeding the flock. Those who are sickly you have not
> strengthened, the diseased you have not healed, the broken
> you have not bound up, the scattered you have not brought
> back, nor have you sought for the lost; but with force and with
> severity you have dominated them.*
>
> —34:2–4

What an indictment of a worthless minister!

The Ends of Preaching

For preaching to be passionate, it must proceed from a heart of compassion that desires to produce Christlikeness in the lives of his hearers. There is a high and holy purpose in his sermon; he will do some good—he *must* do some good—or his flock will suffer. Hence, every sermon should include one or more of the following ends.

1. *We should strive to convert the sinner.* Souls are under the

sentence of condemnation. Baxter says, "Oh, then, for the Lord's sake, and for the sake of poor souls, have pity on them, and bestir yourselves, and spare no pains that may conduce to their salvation."[7] Every sermon should have the gospel. It should end at the cross and the empty tomb.

2. *We should strive to correct the ignorant.* Our generation is biblically illiterate and morally bankrupt as a result. Our sermons should make clear the way of the Lord and instruct them in the good and straight ways of God.

3. *We should strive to reprove the wayward.* The shepherd carries a staff to prod and pull; so should our sermons be equipped with arguments and reminders to those who know the ways of God but choose to go astray. Sermons should correct and convict! Making the wayward uncomfortable in his journey is the sign of a good sermon.

4. *We should strive to heal the broken.* Preaching should not only afflict but also heal. The shepherd's balm should be in the sermon. Every soul is in need, even those who will not recognize it (cf. Rev. 3:17–18). A preacher who will not address the brokenhearted—those whose lives are mangled by sin, whose homes are silent from death or divorce—such a person is not worthy of an audience. It is no wonder that such a preacher ends up with no audience, or with a few scattered, pitiful sheep.

5. *We should strive to teach the simple.* Dr. J. Vernon McGee made it his ambition to "lay the cookies on the lower shelf." Is it any wonder that he, being dead, still speaks? Most of the people in the world are simple, that is, they do not readily grasp deep truths. Yet we preach as though they are seminarians and scholars.

6. *We should strive to inspire the weary.* The world and the church are overrun by tired people, and our hurried culture takes its toll on the best of us. We need a word of encouragement, a call to remembrance of what we already know, a fresh glimpse of heaven, of the glories of Christ, of forgiveness, of the joy of the Holy Spirit. Our sermons should be models of inspiration, breathing life into a spiritless congregation. This

ranting and scolding, this verbal whipping—these will not enhance the kingdom of God. If the world afflicts our people with
cords, shall we do so with scorpions? Is it any wonder that they
flee to their own tents?

7.   *We should strive to protect the helpless.* Our Lord saw us as
     "distressed and downcast, like sheep without a shepherd"
     (Matt. 9:36). Sheep need protection, and our sermons should
     protect them from heresies, from variant teachings, from in-
     ward dissension, from self-destructive habits and sins, and
     from the lure of the world and the schemes of the devil. The
     Word is the sword of the Spirit, and preachers should make
     good use of it to combat the savage wolves that would devour
     the flock of God. The flaming sword in the pulpit—wielded
     skillfully—will effectively guard the entrance into the
     sheepfold.

Preacher, be caught up with the good of your people, and forget
about the good of your sermon. Forget about idolizing methodologies,
expository versus textual, and topical versus narrative. Do not let these
become the main purpose behind your preaching. Rather, mimic the
biblical preachers. Aim at forming Christ in the lives of your people.
Keep the end in mind, *always!*

Gaining Compassion

The question that occupies us in this last segment is, "How does
one gain compassion for people?" Compassion is neither natural nor
universal. Some people are more compassionate than others. Natural
temperaments affect one's compassion as does our environment. If we
were in some other occupation, we could rely upon these two reeds
to excuse our insensitivity. But the misery of those around us and the
charge to assist them challenges all of us to gain a large measure of
compassion! Let us proceed to give some practical ways to enlarge our
hearts toward others.

How to Gain Compassion

- ▶ Study your own heart.
- ▶ Live among the people.
- ▶ Be a careful observer.
- ▶ Read about people.
- ▶ Listen to the heart's cry.
- ▶ Learn from personal trials.

To preach to a human heart, we must understand it. Preachers ignorant of people are like hunters ignorant of their game. We earn the right to speak when we have labored to understand our people. Our effectiveness in communication multiplies when our people can say, "My preacher understands my circumstances; he speaks to my needs." The psalmist extols God for the mercies and benefits given him by his loving God, and the consolation he receives is from his awareness that God knows him and understands his plight. He says of God, "Just as a father has compassion on his children, so the LORD has compassion on those who fear Him. For He Himself knows our frame; He is mindful that we are but dust" (Ps. 103:13–14).

How, then, do we gain such insight into the human heart?

1. *Study your own heart.* The three books readily available to us are the Bible, nature, and our heart. "Know yourself" was a Greek axiom! The homiletical manual also reads, "Know your heart! Be open to yourself, be honest! Understand your weaknesses, desires, temptations, and failings! Face yourself in the mirror of your life, and when you can see your face clearly, then you will see that your face resembles every other face in the world. Then you will understand that every soul proceeds from a common source, the same Maker." A delusional preacher will preach a sermon fit for "extraterrestrials."

   Once you rightly understand who you are and what you need, apply the spiritual meat to your own lean soul. As a newborn babe, you, too, imbibe of the sincere milk of the word (1 Peter 2:1–2). Then form a sermon that preaches to you, to your needs, to your weaknesses, and to your desires. You will rarely miss the bull's eye! I have often been accused of preaching to specific people in my congregation. The truth is, I was preaching to myself. The sermon was primarily for me!

The lost art of meditation has robbed us of this necessary ingredient in the study and assimilation of God's Word. *Meditation is that act of personal application.* Personal introspection and application of God's Word is the greatest discovery of who we really are! We learn more about humanity from the study of self than from any earthly book written on that subject.

2. *Live among the people.* The incarnation of the preacher is indispensable to the ministry of the Word, just as the incarnation of our Savior was essential to His high priestly ministry (cf. Heb. 2:17; 4:15). We learn to be merciful when we, too, encounter the miseries of our people. We learn to sympathize with their weaknesses when we, too, are beset by their trials and tempted by their environments. The man who moves from the Christian cradle to the Christian pulpit without traveling through the valley of tears will never know how rightly to apply the Word to his hearers. He cannot distinguish between the trivialities and the essentials, the urgent and the superfluous, the priority and the peripheral. What a tragedy!

It helps the minister if he has had secular employment, if he lives in the neighborhood of his people, if he shops where they shop, and if his children play with their children. There is here a great argument for the visitation of your people in their homes and places of employment. When you see under what conditions the people live, it will affect what and how you speak. Someone has well said, "Do not criticize a man's walk until you have traveled two miles in his shoes!"

We ministers today are guilty of *aloofness.* We have carried our separation to the extreme. We live in isolation, so isolated that we have lost touch with reality. We think that the masses today pack our churches to know the dimensions of the tabernacle and to decipher the color of its curtains. It may have been true in days gone by, but in today's world, that is far from what they need or want to hear. Their lives are in crisis, and they need someone who understands them. *Do you?*

3. *Carefully observe people.* Preachers must be people-watchers, just as dentists are teeth-observers. We can learn much about people simply by developing a curiosity about them. Here is an area that we cannot avoid. My dentist watches my teeth, but I watch his soul. Others are too preoccupied with their own lives to care much for mine, but my calling makes me "my brother's keeper." I must be on the lookout for them.

   There are places where you can study people: the airport, the playground, the schoolyard, and the very pews in which they sit. There is no place where humans tread where the preacher cannot learn something about them. I heard of a prcacher who wept at a football stadium while thousands of people cheered at the game. They were involved in the action on the field, but he was involved in their lives of desperation. That, friend, is compassion!

4. *Read about people.* The tabloids are proof that people like to know about people. People are interesting, exciting, and challenging. So we read about them. Great preachers are all readers of biographies, from which they glean not only ideas for themselves but also insights into what made such people tick. A good biography is a help in understanding people.

   You need to vary the material you read. Most preachers like biographies of ministers, missionaries, and great Christians. This is good, but we need to expand our selection to include the rank and file prospective parishioner. Their lives are quite distinct from our heroes. Sometimes a movie about a person may serve the same purpose. Although television tends to stereotype people, some programs and movies open the human heart to us. Avail yourself of these resources.

5. *Listen to the heart cry.* Preachers love to talk but have trouble listening. They want others to pay attention to every word they speak but have trouble paying attention to the conversations of others. It is one thing to listen to someone's words; it is quite

another to listen to their heart's cry. Behind those nice re-
marks—those, "I'm doing just fine, pastor"—may be a heart
crying out for help and compassion.

A wise preacher once said, "Be kind to everyone because everyone is having a hard time." How true that is. As I observe
people file into the sanctuary on Sunday mornings, take their
seats, and prepare to worship, I am continually made aware of
the hurts they endure and the burdens they bear. Most endure
them stoically, not letting on that they have these concerns.
They are but a second away from weeping if some careful, concerned soul would simply take a loving interest in their lives.
Unfortunately, we have not learned the art of listening to the
silent scream of the soul in anguish.

A Reality Check

There have been times in my ministry when an icy chill has come
over my heart, when my soul no longer weeps, when my sermons no
longer connect, and when the act of preaching becomes a drudgery. I
know that I have then lost compassion for people. That is when I re-
treat to a small taco stand in the barrio of East Los Angeles, to a place
where real people live. I order a cup of coffee and sit with my back
against the wall. Then I watch, I observe, I read, and I listen intently
for the heart cry.

A group of gang-bangers come in for a snack—one in four will die
before the age of eighteen; two of the others will end up in prison. All
are doomed to a hard life. A young mother comes in with her brood of
youngsters. It is obvious that they are poor. They share drinks. They
live in poverty; some will never see a forest or snow. An old drunk
staggers in, begging for a meal. He is quickly thrown out. That was
somebody's baby boy. A mother at one time cradled that man and
nursed him. The poor specimen of humanity has children. His wife is
somewhere out there. They have long since disowned him, but they
have not forgotten him. He is still somebody's daddy. For all I know,
he could have been my own.

I look, I listen until I hear their cries, until their souls cry out to me, "Please help, I'm perishing!" until the tears pour forth from my melted heart! I am in love with humanity once again. Now I am fit to ascend the pulpit, to weep with those who weep, to laugh with those who laugh, and to bring a living Word—Christ—to a needy people. Now I can preach with passion, for now I have compassion.

4

Preach with Authority

The result was that when Jesus had finished these words, the multitudes were amazed at His teaching; for He was teaching them as one having authority, and not as their scribes.
—Matthew 7:28–29

The greatest sermon ever preached, the Sermon on the Mount, brought the audience to astonishment. The Scriptures testify that the crowds "were amazed at His teaching; for He was teaching them as one having authority, and not as their scribes" (Matt. 7:28–29). Luke states that they "were continually amazed at His teaching, for His message was with authority" (Luke 4:32). The Lord Jesus left His audience in prolonged amazement because of *what* and *how* He spoke. William Hendriksen attributes the impact of the Lord's teaching on these principles:

1. Jesus spoke the truth (John 14:6; 18:37), whereas the scribes had corrupt and evasive reasoning (Matt. 5:21ff.).
2. Jesus presented matters of life, death, and eternity, whereas the scribes spoke on trivialities (Matt. 23:23; Luke 11:23).
3. There was a system in Jesus' teaching, whereas the scribes rambled on and on.
4. Jesus excited curiosity by making generous use of illustrations (Matt. 5:13–16; 6:26–30; 7:24–27) and concrete examples (Matt. 5:21–6:24), whereas the sermons of the scribes were dry and boring.
5. Jesus spoke as the Lover of people, pointing to the Father's love for people (Matt. 5:44–48), whereas the scribes lacked love in their teaching (Matt. 23:4, 13–15).
6. Jesus spoke with authority, for His message came from the Father (John 8:26), from His inner being, and from the Scriptures (Matt. 5:17; 7:12; cf. 4:4, 7, 10), whereas the scribes used fallible sources and one another.[1]

The Lord spoke with "authoritative power."[2] But such authoritative teaching with authority was not just a onetime occurrence. This was His lifelong way of teaching and preaching. What a contrast with the teaching of His day! The teaching of the scribes was

> at once erudite and foolish, at once contemptuous and mean; never passing a hair's breadth beyond the carefully watched boundary line of commentary and precedent; full of balanced

inference, and orthodox hesitancy, and impossible literalism;
intricate with legal pettiness and labyrinthine system; elevat-
ing mere memory above genius, and repetitions above origi-
nality; concerned only about priests and Pharisees, in Temple
and synagogue, or school, or Sanhedrin, and mostly occupied
with things, infinitely little. It was not, indeed, wholly devoid of moral significance, nor is it impossible to find here
and there among the debris of it a noble thought; but it was
occupied a thousand fold more with Levitical minutiae about
mint, and anise, and cummin, and the length of fringes, and
the breadth of phylacteries, and the washing of cups, and plat-
ters, and the particular quarter of a second when the new
moons and Sabbaths began.[3]

Such describes some of our modern-day preaching. We need to ask
ourselves, "Does my preaching resemble that of the scribes, filled with
tangents and trivia, or is it like the Lord's, focused on the weighty and
meaty truths of eternity?" The question is vital to our preaching with
passion. "Trivial pursuit" in preaching leads to anemic preaching, no
matter how much we excite ourselves!

> *"Teaching with authority is learned*
> *from Christ—not from the scribes."*

Teaching with authority is learned from Christ, not from the
scribes. Even today, "Christian scribes" influence much of our preaching. We look to psychology, to history, to current events, and to com-
mentaries to verify our message. No wonder it lacks authority. I like
what John Broadus states in his commentary on Matthew 7:28:

It is the part of wisdom, as well as of modesty, to give no
small weight to the opinions of men whose abilities, learning, and piety have made them illustrious; but if a man is not
accustomed to come for himself to the Bible, and form his

own judgment of its meaning, his teachings, whatever else they may possess, will have little of living power to sway men's souls.[4]

We need to "preach the Word," not what people *say* about the Word. Authority lies in the Word of God, not in the teachings of men of renown!

> **au•thor•i•ty** *n.* the power to determine, adjudicate, or otherwise settle issues; a power or right delegated or given; authorization.[5]

Authority, Not Authoritarianism

Preaching with authority is not readily comprehended by everyone. Some mistake authority for *authoritarianism*. They see authority as power, control, and total influence. Some preachers turn into "little popes," spiritual dictators who turn the pulpit into a throne, the church into their kingdom, and the Bible into a manipulation tool. Indeed, some of our churches border on being cultic, following in the footsteps of the cults in trying to control the church through the pulpit.

The Lord Jesus aptly described what it does *not* mean to teach and preach with authority. It all has to do with how we view the people and the type of relationship we have with them. The Savior said to His disciples when they confused their roles:

> *You know that the rulers of the Gentiles lord it over them, and their great men exercise authority over them. It is not so among you, but whoever wishes to become great among you shall be your servant, and whoever wishes to be first among you shall be your slave; just as the Son of Man did not come to be served, but to serve, and to give His life a ransom for many.*
>
> —Matthew 20:25–28

The apostle Peter also admonishes all preachers that to preach with authority is not to be confused with "lording it over" the people (1 Peter 5:1–4). The pulpit is an extremely hazardous place. Neophytes especially can become conceited (1 Tim. 3:6). Pastors may use their preaching as a whip to keep people in line, to quell opposition! It is indeed tragic and sad when a preacher turns "bully" in his pulpit.

How to Preach with Authority

So what does it mean to preach with authority? We shall see that to preach authoritatively—and therefore passionately—one must speak as follows.

Preaching with Authority

▶ Speak as a believer.
▶ Speak as an ambassador.
▶ Speak as a saint.
▶ Speak as a scholar.
▶ Speak as a skillful artist.

1. *Speak as a believer*. The authority possessed by personal experience is unsurpassed. Nothing can equal the words, "I know it is true—it happened to me!" A true believer will be passionate about what he believes, even if the object of that belief is false or unwarranted (note the followers of Jim Jones or the kamikaze pilots under the Imperial Japanese Army).

The power of apostolic preaching can be traced to this principle: *"I believe; therefore I speak!"* The apostle Paul lays this principle as the reason why he and his companions could endure unspeakable sufferings and deprivations: they knew Christ and had a personal experience with Him. There was no denying it! Listen to Paul:

> But we have this treasure in earthen vessels, that the surpassing greatness of the power may be of God and not from ourselves; we are afflicted in every way, but not crushed;

perplexed, but not despairing; persecuted, but not forsaken;
struck down, but not destroyed; always carrying about in the
body the dying of Jesus, that the life of Jesus also may be
manifested in our body. For we who live are constantly be-
ing delivered over to death for Jesus' sake, that the life of Jesus
also may be manifested in our mortal flesh. So death works
in us, but life in you. But having the same spirit of faith, ac-
cording to what is written, "I believed, therefore I spoke," we
also believe, therefore also we speak; knowing that He who
raised the Lord Jesus will raise us also with Jesus and will
present us with you.

—2 Corinthians 4:7–14

That is passionate living! That is passionate, authoritative preaching! It proceeds from a personal faith in a risen Savior and firm confidence in the resurrection to life!

The passionate preaching of the apostles came from their speaking
as believers. They were eyewitnesses of the glories of Christ. Peter
asserts, "For we did not follow cleverly devised tales when we made
known to you the power and coming of our Lord Jesus Christ, but we
were eyewitnesses of His majesty" (2 Peter 1:16). Peter was there! He
saw; he heard!

Twice the apostles were commanded by the Jewish rulers to cease
from proclaiming the gospel of Christ, but the unlettered men would
not be silenced. Peter and John boldly responded, "Whether it is right
in the sight of God to give heed to you rather than God, you be the
judge; for we cannot stop speaking about what we have seen and heard"
(Acts 4:19–20). They believed, therefore they spoke! Some time later,
the same prohibition was pressed upon them by the Jewish Council,
and again they authoritatively responded, "We must obey God rather
than men" (Acts 5:29). Ultimately, the reason for this boldness and
authority came because they were "witnesses of these things" (5:32).
Again, they saw and therefore spoke.

Even ignorance and poverty, when armed with faith, is a conqueror
over erudition and power when incredulous. Witness the blind man
given his sight in John 9. After much interrogation and badgering by

the Jewish authorities, the man who was made to see could not be made to deny what had happened to him. His recourse was the same: "Whether He is a sinner, I do not know; one thing I do know, that whereas I was blind, now I see" (John 9:25). He grew even bolder as the interrogation continued. His final statement came with great authority as he passionately refuted his antagonists (cf. John 9:30–33). Here was an ignorant man who because of personal experience put to shame the "reasoning of the wise." We see the authority that belief gives to one!

The case for personal belief in what we preach is obvious. You cannot speak passionately or authoritatively about what you do not personally and wholeheartedly believe. Every truth found in Scripture needs to be filtered through our being until it takes root and yields faith. If you truly believe something, you will speak passionately upon that issue. You may not know all there is to know about a certain subject, but you will say like Paul, "I believe, therefore I speak."

> *"You cannot speak passionately or authoritatively about what you do not personally and wholeheartedly believe."*

The weakness of liberalism and contemporary evangelicalism tainted with the undermining doubts of modernism is that it erodes confidence in the Scriptures. A "doubting Thomas" cannot speak confidently about a risen Savior. But when the issue about the inspiration, veracity, and authority of Scripture is settled in a preacher's soul, when he believes that "all Scripture is inspired by God and profitable" (2 Tim. 3:16), then he can proceed to preach the Word with total authority.

I have often said that if the Bible is not God's inerrant, infallible Word in its entirety, I must seek another vocation, for how can I preach a lie to others? I would be a double cheat. The fact is that the Bible *is* the Word of God, so we can preach it with authority. Therein was the authority of Christ: He preached the Holy Scriptures with authority because He believed them to be *truth;* "the Scriptures cannot be broken!" (John 10:35). No man who fills the sacred desk should have a lesser view of Scripture!

2. *Speak as an ambassador.* Our authority lies not in ourselves, but in God. We are actually His ambassadors, speaking in His stead, just as Paul states: "Therefore, we are ambassadors for Christ, as though God were entreating through us; we beg you on behalf of Christ, be reconciled to God" (2 Cor. 5:20).

Paul called himself an "ambassador in chains" (Eph. 6:20), for he himself knew that his ministry was one in which he was first chosen by Christ and then sent to a particular people (cf. Acts 9:15).

Characteristics of an Ambassador

- ▶ Sent as an envoy
- ▶ Sent in place of someone else; a representative
- ▶ Sent with the authority of the one who sent him
- ▶ Sent to speak and act with that authority

In much the same way, every preacher is an ambassador for Christ. We must speak as His ambassadors. Our commission is not one we chose or we took up as some whim or fancy. We did not even "volunteer" to become preachers of the Word. The office is for those who are *divinely* called! To do otherwise is to fall under the indictment of God: "I have neither sent them nor commanded them nor spoken to them" (Jer. 14:14). Contrast this with the ministry of those sent by God. Jeremiah was such an ambassador, sent by God to the house of Israel. Note his conduct:

> Then Jeremiah came from Topheth, where the LORD had sent him to prophesy; and he stood in the court of the LORD's house and said to all the people: "Thus says the LORD of hosts, the God of Israel, 'Behold, I am about to bring on this city and all its towns the entire calamity that I have declared against it, because they have stiffened their necks so as not to heed My words'" (Jer. 19:14–15).

The reluctant prophet had to deliver the message because God sent him; he had no choice or say in the matter. The same can be said about Ezekiel (cf. Ezek. 3:4–6) and the rest of the prophets. Even the apostles were "sent men" (cf. Matt. 10:1; 28:18–20; John 17:18; 20:21), and they faithfully represented their Lord on this earth. They were His ambassadors then, as we also are today.

As ambassadors of God, we should speak with authority. Our common refrain should be "Thus says the Lord," "The Scriptures say," and "The Bible says!" We declare Christ's words, not our own. Neither should we be afraid to address any person or any crowd with the truth. Apply to yourself God's words to Titus: "These things speak and exhort and reprove with all authority. Let no one disregard you" (Titus 2:15).

I fear that we are much too apologetic as preachers. It seems as if we speak more like door-to-door salesmen—peddling our gospel wares—than as ambassadors of Christ declaring forth the gospel message. We need to be more like Ehud, who declared, "I have a message from God for you" (Judg. 3:20). In short, "I'm not asking if you want it, nor if you like it, nor if you agree with it, nor to debate it. Neither am I asking if you deny it. I'm simply delivering it to you with all of the passion and urgency and authority that it demands. What you do with it is your responsibility. You must reckon with God for this message, not with me!"

Listen to what Lloyd-Jones says, and dare never to be wishy-washy again:

> The preacher should never be apologetic, he should never give the impression that he is speaking by their leave as it were; he should not be tentatively putting forward certain suggestions and ideas. That is not to be his attitude at all. He is a man, who is there to "declare" certain things; he is a man under commission and under authority. He is an ambassador, and he should be aware of his authority. He should always know that he comes to the congregation as a sent messenger.[6]

Hence, as an ambassador,

- preach the Word of God *authoritatively,* and use the expression, "Thus saith the Lord";
- preach to represent your Lord *authentically* (cf. 1 Cor. 4:1–4);
- preach in the *second person;* do not be afraid to say, "you!";
- preach to *apply the text;* a prophet speaks to his generation (cf. Luke 3:10–14);
- preach for a *personal* and *visible response;* refuse to let people "hesitate between two opinions" (cf. 1 Kings 18:21);
- preach to be *clearly understood* and not to please the audience; and
- preach *fearlessly* and *flawlessly;* don't let the messenger influence the message negatively (cf. 1 Tim. 4:11–16; 2 Cor. 13:10).

3. *Speak as a saint.* The preacher's authority increases with age if his life draws nearer and nearer to Christlikeness. I marvel at the power and authority of older pastors. I have noticed that two men can preach identical sermons—the young one may receive the applause, but the old preacher gets the attention. What is the difference? The life of Christ formed more thoroughly in the life of the older preacher.

The mistake made by many young preachers is that they attempt to mimic the style of great, older preachers, but they fail to mimic their lives as well. The latter gives the former its power. First we sanctify the man, who in turn sanctifies the style. If we would make it our ambition to know Christ more intimately, we would preach Christ more powerfully. Authority comes when the glory of Christ surrounds our lives, even as in the case of Moses on his descent from Mount Sinai (cf. Exod. 34:28–35). Paul's advice to young Timothy was to strive to be what he preached, knowing that the more of the Word the man has in his life, the more life there will be in his spoken word. Consider his words with "saintliness" in mind:

> *Prescribe and teach these things. Let no one look down on your youthfulness, but rather in speech, conduct, love, faith and purity, show yourself an example of those who believe. . . . Take pains with these things; be absorbed in them, so that your progress may be evident to all. Pay close*

attention to yourself and to your teaching; persevere in these things; for as you do this you will insure salvation both for yourself and for those who hear you.
                                                    —1 Timothy 4:11–12, 15–16

And,

Flee from these things, you man of God, and pursue righteousness, godliness, faith, love, perseverance and gentleness.
                                                    —1 Timothy 6:11

And again,

Now in a large house there are not only gold and silver vessels, but also vessels of wood and of earthenware, and some to honor and some to dishonor. Therefore, if a man cleanses himself from these things, he will be a vessel for honor, sanctified, useful to the Master, prepared for every good work. Now flee from youthful lusts, and pursue righteousness, faith, love and peace, with those who call on the Lord from a pure heart.
                                                    —2 Timothy 2:20–22

A preacher's authority should increase with the length of his ministry only because he has learned to practice what he preaches. It is this aspect of the preacher that John Maxwell terms "personhood": *a person who embodies the message he proclaims.*[7]

Maxwell's Levels of Leadership[8]

- ▶ **Position:** authority because of one's job description.
- ▶ **Permission:** empowering others to actions.
- ▶ **Production:** authority because of a successful track record.
- ▶ **People Development:** earned respect from others because of what you have done for them.
- ▶ **Personhood:** embodiment of what you teach over a lifetime.

The longer one walks with Christ and the longer one stays in the same ministry, the more authority rests on him.

If we would be saints in our ministry, we must

- strive for holiness in the *total man;*
- understand that *holiness is a process,* growing in grace and in the knowledge of Christ;
- let our trials *purge our imperfections;*
- avoid the *blunders of youth;*
- avoid the *foolishness of our older years;*
- plan for *long ministry* in the same place; and
- let authority *grow with the years.*

4. *Speak as a scholar.* If one is an expert in his field, then he is also considered an authority. Television commercials have captured this fact. You will notice how people of the medical profession promote pain relievers. Even superstars are made promoters of everything from hamburgers to household cleaners. We listen to authorities!

The same holds true for preaching. If a preacher knows his subject well, if he has mastered it, if he has become an authority on it, then he will speak confidently about it, even passionately. But if he is unsure of his subject or his field, he will speak hesitantly, perhaps reluctantly, and certainly not very authoritatively. There are times when we may bluff our way through a subject, but sooner or later the people will find out that we are simply a well-articulated windbag, with no real substance.

The ministry of the great preacher-orator Apollos was made even more powerful by the careful instruction of Aquila and Priscilla (cf. Acts 18:24–28). Apollos was already a passionate preacher (cf. 18:25), but he lacked some substance. Yet when he was instructed, his preaching became even more powerful (v. 28). "It is the truly informed preacher who commands the respect of the people," argues James Cox.[9]

A preacher is a man of one book, the Bible, of which he must be the authority. He must know the Bible backward and forward. He must understand its content and be able to declare and defend its truths. The preacher is a man of one profession, the overseer of the people of

God. He must know how to shepherd God's flock. It is well to know other disciplines. It is good to be well-read in fields of literature, and it is relevant to his ministry to be up on the times in which he lives. But he does not need to be an authority in those areas. However, when it comes to the Bible, theology, and the ministry, he is to have no equal in the congregation. This is his specialty. Here he is the authority, and it is his scholarship that lends power to his preaching.

Let me add that many of our sermons are delivered with less than passionate authority because we are unfamiliar with the text we are expositing, or because we are unfamiliar with the arrangement and flow of the sermon. It was said of George Whitefield that you could always tell when he had a new sermon, for it lacked authoritative power in its delivery. But let Whitefield master the sermon, and he soon moved the audience under his preaching.

A few questions are in order here. Do we study to understand and master the biblical text? Have we properly constructed the sermon so that by its very form it guarantees a ready acceptance? Have we read extensively on the subject we seek to address? Are we so familiar with the contents and form of our sermon, that if we lost the manuscript or our notes, we could deliver it extemporaneously and with great effect?

5. *Speak as a skillful artist.* Preaching is an art, not just an act. Congregations have long moved beyond the simple lecture on the Bible and the "sharing a few nuggets" from the Word. Every area of Christendom has moved into the next stage of its development. Music, Sunday school, buildings, sound systems, lighting, and church offices—all these have progressed to a level above mediocrity.

The same expectation is held for the preacher. The people have gathered to worship where the pianist is skilled, where the soloist has perfected her voice, where the choir has rehearsed their cantata, and where the architect has yielded the fruit of his profession. Then in comes the preacher, who has not given his delivery a second thought! He blunders through an unprepared introduction, reads through his notes, and crash lands an unfinished sermon because his "time was up." Do you expect people to respond kindly to this contrast?

We owe it to God and to our people to be skillful in our preaching, from its exegesis to its exposition. Timothy Turner warns us in his book *Preaching to Programmed People* that we preachers are in steep competition with a world trained in communication and with a people accustomed to skillful communicators. He states, "TV competes with preaching in the business of communication. In fact, any preacher not in the communication business goes out of business."[10] A preacher today cannot be any less skilled in his art of preaching than his competitors are in the art of communication.

Proverbs 22:29 says, "Do you see a man skilled in his work? He will stand before kings; he will not stand before obscure men." God honors a skilled preacher! He grants him to speak with authority without blotting out the glory of God! Developing our skill in preaching does not invalidate the power of God any less than properly trimming the sails in one's boat annuls the power of the wind. Nay, it enhances it. Preacher, would you preach passionately? *Then prepare!*

The Challenge

We have seen here that passionate preaching is one that preaches with authority. An authoritarian preacher has no place in the pulpit, but then neither does a man lacking authority, a man not sent from God. Hence, my dear brother, preach authoritatively, by

- speaking as a true believer in what you preach,
- speaking as one sent from God,
- speaking as a venerable saint who knows God,
- speaking as an authority on your subject, and
- speaking as one trained to persuade and convince.

Be like Ehud: "I have a message from God for you!" (Judg. 3:20).

5

Preach with Urgency

And with many other words he solemnly testified and kept on exhorting them, saying, "Be saved from this perverse generation!"

—Acts 2:40

P assionate preaching is preaching with urgency. If your neighbor's house was engulfed in flames, and you awoke at midnight to the inferno, knowing that your neighbors were in the house, you would surely react in earnest. You would make an urgent plea to the fire department and would make an urgent effort to save those inside the house. You would respond passionately to the situation.

The spiritual house is no different. Souls are in desperate need of help. The world, the flesh, and the devil are wreaking havoc upon the souls of people! The eternal fire that threatens to consume them is deadlier than any temporal conflagration. There is a sense of urgency all around us. How can we be listless and apathetic?

> **ur•gent** *adj.* compelling or re-
> quiring immediate action or
> attention; imperative;
> pressing; insistent or ear-
> nest in solicitation; impor-
> tunate.[1]

Preaching thus becomes *sanctified madness*. The preacher is beside himself. He is a lunatic, a madman, for the dangers of the human soul drive the watchman to a sanctified frenzy as he tries to warn sinners of their plight. Christ was accused of madness (cf. John 10:20), as were the apostles (cf. 2 Cor. 5:13). Paul was especially accused of insanity (cf. Acts 26:25). Yet such were not mentally deranged madmen, just men thoroughly filled with a deep sense of urgency. David Eby writes,

> Preaching today is so often passive, apathetic, impotent, soft, spineless and lame. It lacks fervor, heat, and heart. It is passionateless. What can turn preaching around? What can restore fire-breathing, white-hot power preaching in our day? The answer is quite simple. Preachers must become gospel maniacs. Preachers must become captivated and re-captivated by the Lord Jesus Christ and the gospel. No intoxication for

the gospel, no mania for the good news means no fire. No fire means no power preaching![2]

The apostle Paul was a passionate preacher because he had a sense of urgency about him. He was held captive by his commission and by his compassion. Paul knew that people were utterly lost without Christ. He was a driven preacher! In the apostle's defense before King Agrippa, Festus accused him of being crazy (Acts 26:24). Paul proceeded to insist upon his declaration and to plead with them to repent, so that even the king came near repentance, saying, "In a short time you will persuade me to become a Christian" (Acts 26:28). Paul was urgent about his message.

We need urgency in our preaching, but why don't we have it? Is the following accusation applicable to us?

> Have we become so careless, so criminally familiar with such topics as salvation and damnation, that we can descant upon them with the same calmness, coolness, not to say indifference, with which a public lecturer will discuss a branch of natural philosophy?[3]

The great pastor Richard Baxter said, "How many sleep under us, because our hearts and tongues are sleepy, and we bring not with us so much skill and zeal as to awaken them!"[4] And it is with a sense of urgency that Jude states, "And have mercy on some, who are doubting; save others, snatching them out of the fire; and on some have mercy with fear, hating even the garment polluted by the flesh (Jude 22–23). Clearly, the biblical watchword is *urgency!* The historian Luke says of Peter's preaching at Pentecost, "And with many other words he solemnly testified and kept on exhorting them, saying, 'Be saved from this perverse generation!'" (Acts 2:40). No wonder thousands came to Christ after such preaching!

We shall learn to preach urgently and never be accused of complacency and compromise when we keep four guidelines before us.

Preaching with Urgency

▶ Preach with judgment in mind.
▶ Preach toward a verdict.
▶ Preach for the uniqueness of the moment.
▶ Preach under divine sovereignty.

Preach with Judgment in Mind

The threat of punishment is a great motivator. The presence of danger always makes us alter our direction in life. The impending harm upon our fellowmen should move us to help them, should compel us to warn them, to turn them, to snatch them away from danger. Our dancing with psychological Delilahs and liberal Jezebels has taken the sting out of sin and hell! Sin is considered a disease and eternal punishment a myth, neither eternal nor a punishment! Therefore, fire that does not burn is not to be feared, and transgressions that do not sting are not a curse. No wonder the average pulpit has no ring of urgency.

The true biblical preacher knows differently. He understands both the sting of sin and the horrors of hell. Hence, he preaches with the near judgment of sin before him, and the final judgment of hell on the horizon! Urgency is in his voice. His steps are quickened by the necessity of rescuing souls! There is no time to waste!

1. *Preach with the near judgment of sin in mind.* Sin is an enemy of God and of us. Yet, although sin is our mortal enemy, people pursue it, take pleasure in it, revel in it, and protect it as one would protect a pet cobra—unaware that it is really no one's pet. Sin may lie in your bosom but will strike at you when you least expect it. If people only knew the great evil of sin, and if people only knew the danger and harm brought about by it!

Why Sin Is to Be Feared

▶ Sin is satanic (1 John 3:8).
▶ Sin is lawlessness (1 John 3:4).

▶ Sin is a passing pleasure (Heb. 11:25).

▶ Sin deceives (Heb. 3:13).

▶ Sin entangles (Heb. 12:1).

▶ Sin enslaves (John 8:34).

▶ Sin hardens (Heb. 3:13).

▶ Sin stings (1 Cor. 15:56).

▶ Sin kills (Rom. 5:12).

▶ Sin damns (1 Cor. 6:9).

Sin is the mortal enemy of mankind. Sin destroys the life and damns the soul. Sin entices with pleasure only to sting with death. No one has escaped or ever will escape the effects of sin. We are *conceived* in sin, *commit* sin, and are doomed to *continue* in sin unless the grace of Christ intervenes. Ultimately, we will be *condemned* by sin to hell if the blood of the cross does not cleanse us from it. The only hope for sinful humanity is the cross. Only the Lamb of God can take away the sin of the world (John 1:29). I must continually remind myself and my people that sin is no friend of ours!

Sin has names! It can easily be identified if we stick to its biblical definitions and if we call it by its real names. Our Lord spoke of sin as that which defiles a person, as that which proceeds from within, and He identified it by name:

> *For from within, out of the heart of men, proceed the evil thoughts, fornications, thefts, murders, adulteries, deeds of coveting and wickedness, as well as deceit, sensuality, envy, slander, pride and foolishness. All these evil things proceed from within and defile the man.*
>
> —Mark 7:21–23

We should be ready to call sin by name, as the apostle Paul did in Romans 1:28–32, 1 Corinthians 6:9–11, and Galatians 5:19–21! Modernity is enamored with the practice of redefining sin and calling evil good and good evil (cf. Isa. 5:20). God forbid that we should water down the sinfulness of sin, for then we would be sorry physicians of the soul.

A certain man was asked what the preacher spoke about in the service that Sunday. "He spoke about sin," was his reply. "Well, and what did he say about it?" came back the question. The man tersely responded, "He said he was against it." May the same be said of us.

2. *Preach with the final judgment of hell in mind.* The Bible is explicitly clear that a fiery ordeal of eternal punishment awaits the godless and those who do not obey the gospel of our Lord Jesus (cf. 2 Thess. 1:9). The lake of fire is reserved for those who do not have their names inscribed in the Book of Life (cf. Rev. 20:15). The apostles preached with urgency because they knew that a day of reckoning awaits all people and that unbelievers have an eternal doom reserved for them.

We rob preaching of its urgency when we rob hell of its severity and its eternality. If there is no hell, then there needs to be no urgency. But if hell is real, then we must preach in earnest, with urgency. If a person is caught in a raging fire, we would be in earnest to rescue that person from the flames. How much more when a soul is headed to a Christless eternity, to an eternal state of conscious torment.

> ### "We rob preaching of its urgency when we rob hell of its severity."

Our preaching should be an urgent appeal to a lost world. As Lloyd-Jones reminds us,

> You are not simply imparting information, you are dealing with souls, you are dealing with pilgrims on the way to eternity, you are dealing with matters not only of life and death in this world, but with eternal destiny. Nothing can be so terribly urgent.[5]

One preacher said that he always does his hospital visits on Saturday so as to remind himself to preach on Sunday with eternity in view. We should have such an urgency about us as we preach. People should know that we mean business, that we believe in hell, that people without Christ are hell-bound, and that the gospel is their only hope! Listen to Spurgeon again:

> It is an observation of pious Mr. Baxter (which I have read somewhere in his works), that he has never known any considerable success from the brightest and noblest talents, nor from the most excellent kind of preaching, nor even when the preachers themselves have been truly religious, if they have not had a solicitous concern for the success of their ministrations. Let the awful and important thought of souls being saved by our preaching, or left to perish and to be condemned to hell through our negligence . . . dwell ever upon our spirits.[6]

The judgment of God upon sin is a sobering thought. Paul would say, "Knowing the fear of the Lord, we persuade men" (2 Cor. 5:11). Jude says, "Save others, snatching them out of the fire" (Jude 23). Judgment is what preachers nowadays avoid, but judgment is what we all need to hear about. Judgment was central to apostolic preaching (e.g., Acts 17:31; 24:25). Let it be central to your preaching. In a day of "seeker sensitive" preaching, be sinner sensitive! Be judgment sensitive! Tell them what awaits them if they do not repent (cf. Heb. 10:26–31).

Preach Toward a Verdict

A second feature that will help us preach with more urgency is to have an expressed purpose in our preaching. I call this *preaching toward a verdict*. My message should have an expressed purpose for its delivery, and I should expect a definite response from my people. Every participant in any activity expects to accomplish something. The baseball pitcher has the strikeout in mind; the batter expects the hit. None of these simply go through the motions. It is to our shame that we preachers can go through the routine of preaching and never expect that our people will do anything with our sermons. We plan no response, so we have no response. And since we expect no response, we do not preach with the urgency to elicit a response!

Even D. Martyn Lloyd-Jones talks of the need to have a verdict when we preach:

> Surely the whole object of this act is to persuade people. The preacher does not just say things with the attitude of "take it or leave it." He desires to persuade them of the truth of his message; he wants them to see it; he is trying to do something to them, to influence them.[7]

Have a reason to preach. Ours is not just to help them understand the truth but to persuade them to be "doers of the word" (James 1:27). Exposition is not merely explaining truth but expecting people to practice truth! Jerry Vines helps us here when he states,

> The preacher who learns to preach from his heart will move men to action. Our purpose is not merely to present a Bible message for the purpose of information or display. We preach in order to bring men to a decision. Our purpose is to change behavior for the better, to bring men to obedience to God, and to lead them to accept the challenge of a Christ-centered life. Heart preaching will help us accomplish those goals. When Cicero spoke to the people it was said, "How well Cicero speaks." But when Demosthenes spoke the people said, "Let us march against Carthage."[8]

Expositors need to keep these words in mind. We are in danger of making "exposition" the end in itself, rather than a means to an end. Paul's exhortation to "preach the word!" is more to accomplish an end (i.e., teaching, reproving, correcting, training, and exhorting) than an act for an act's sake! Although exposition is the chief of methodologies, if it has no verdict, no explicit purpose, and no warrant, then it will lack in pathos and urgency. Since every portion of Scripture has a purpose, the expositor must find that purpose and preach that purpose. Topical or textual preaching must do the same. There must be a reason for the selection of the topic. A verdict must govern the argument and delivery. The same applies to so-called textual preaching. Remember: *Moral action is the active response desired, Christlikeness is the state to be achieved, and God's glory is the overall end of preaching.*

Preaching toward a verdict defies all rules and arrangement in the same way that urgency crosses lines of civility and propriety. The need determines the means! An urgent preacher is very much a madman. An urgent preacher wants you to know something, to do something, to act responsibly, and to act *now!* Preaching with a verdict in mind is urgent preaching and, naturally, passionate preaching.

Consider these piercing words from Baxter:

> If you would prosper in your work, be sure to keep up earnest desires and expectation of success. If your hearts be not set on the end of your labors, and you long not to see the conversion and edification of your hearers, and do not study and preach in hope, you are not likely to see much success. . . . He never had the right ends of a preacher, who is indifferent whether he obtain them, and is not grieved when he misseth them, and rejoiced when he can see the desired issue.[9]

Preach for the Uniqueness of the Moment

Urgency comes when we realize that we may not have another opportunity, when time is running out, and when this may be our last chance. When we think that we have all the time in the world or that our hearers will get another opportunity to hear us again, why should we be in earnest about our preaching? Yet we must preach for the uniqueness of the moment, as though it may be *our* last sermon or as though it may be *their* last sermon.

> *"Every sermon should be preached as though it was our last."*

Every sermon should be preached as though it was our last. We can lull ourselves into complacency by embarking upon a series of messages or by launching into an exposition of a book and wait until the end to preach for the desired results. The truth is, very few of our listeners continue with us consistently until the end. Hence, even in a series of sermons or in an exposition of a book, every sermon should stand by itself (like railroad cars in a train), and we should preach each one as though it was the last sermon we ever preached. In fact, we may never indeed preach again. "I preach," said Baxter, "as never sure to preach again, and as a dying man to dying men."[10] Every sermon is our last will and testament, accompanied by all the seriousness and solemnity that befits it.

We should also preach every sermon as though it were the last sermon our hearers would ever hear this side of eternity. The account of D. L. Moody's words to his audience before the great Chicago fire is legendary. He warned his audience on the Sunday before the fire to think about his words and to return the following week. Many of them did not return—they died in that fire. That affected Moody's preaching! Thereafter, he preached as though the audience would never hear another sermon. We must imitate Moody!

There are many souls who have passed on to a Christless eternity because I thought they had more time. I did not consider their unconverted state urgent enough to warrant any earnestness on my part. They died before I could tell them about Christ. Backsliders were not reclaimed, marriages were not strengthened, and young people were not warned—all because I thought they would be back the next week to hear the conclusion. They did not return. It was their last sermon from me!

> "Speak to your people as to men that must be awakened, either here or in hell! . . . Oh, speak not one cold or careless word about so great a business as heaven or hell. Whatever you do, let the people see that you are in good earnest. . . . Men will not cast away their dearest pleasures at the drowsy request of one that seemeth not to mean as he speaks, or to care much whether his request is granted or not."
>
> —Richard Baxter[11]

I have tried, not always successfully, to preach each sermon as though it were my last and their last. The sermon should be so constructed that it contains all that I want it to say on that particular subject to lead the person to a knowledgeable heart decision, and then I try to deliver it as though it is to be my last. This exercise is tough when you have multiple services back to back. *Yet it must be done!* I have no other option. There may not be a "next time" for them or for me!

Preach Under Divine Sovereignty

Preaching can be guilt producing. The urgency of rescuing the lost coupled with our human weaknesses and limitations can affect us deeply. We are made to live like the mythological Atlas, with the weight of the world upon our shoulders. Man's destiny lies in our hands. They turn or burn based upon zeal or sloth. What a cross to bear!

Our sanity and salvation comes from the precious doctrine of the sovereignty of God, that God is in charge of all things and ultimately responsible for it all. Here is not only the believer's rest but also the preacher's comfort. The preacher works with all his might, but he rests ultimately in the awesome power and perfect will of God. Divine sovereignty is our divine succor!

Yet divine sovereignty improperly understood can yield some unfortunate results. Upon the preacher, it can lead to anxiety or apathy. Anxiety comes to "Arminians" who take all the credit and responsibility for the outcome of their labors. Here is the preacher who has no rest in body or soul because he truly feels that man's eternal destiny depends *entirely* upon what he does. "Woe is me if I do not preach the gospel" (1 Cor. 9:16) is taken to illogical and unscriptural limits.

For certain "Calvinistic" preachers it tends toward apathy. The logic is as follows: "If all is of God, and God's sovereignty works in spite of man, then it does not matter if we labor much for the good of others. In fact, we may be attempting to thwart God's sovereignty by means of our zeal." Hence, urgency in preaching is a lack of true faith and trust in God's power.

Obviously, the matter of God's sovereignty and man's effort meet someplace in the middle; they are "friends," as Spurgeon said. Election, predestination, and divine sovereignty need not excuse us from the urgency of preaching. In fact, these rather are an impetus to zeal in preaching, for one's work has the promise of a sure reward. We labor in hope, and so we labor more intensely. We see this in the case of Paul in Corinth, when his message was met with rejection by the Jews. God encouraged him through a night vision: "Do not be afraid any longer, but go on speaking and do not be silent; for I am with you, and no man will attack you in order to harm you, for I have many people in this city" (Acts 18:9–10). The result was more earnestness on Paul's part and the birth of the Corinthian church (cf. 18:11).

> *"Election, predestination, and divine sovereignty need not excuse us from the urgency of preaching."*

Spurgeon, Whitefield, and other "Calvinistic" preachers are models in this urgency of preaching. They show that election and urgent proclamation are not incompatible. Jonathan Edwards was a true Calvinistic preacher, yet see how urgency and passion flamed his soul. His sermon "Sinners in the Hands of an Angry God" is full of passion and urgency. He believed in affecting the feelings of his hearers. Listen to what he said:

> Sinners should be earnestly invited to come and accept the Savior—with all the winning, encouraging arguments that the Gospel affords. Yet if in these sermons he shall find the most important truths exhibited and pressed home on the conscience with that pungency which tends to awaken, convince, humble and edify; if he shall find that serious strain of piety which, in spite of himself, forces upon him a serious frame of

mind; if in the perusal, he cannot but be ashamed and alarmed at himself, and in some measure feel the reality and weight of eternal things; if, at least he, like Agrippa, shall be almost persuaded to be a Christian; I presume he will not grudge the time required to peruse what is now offered him. These, I mistake not, are the great ends to be aimed at in all sermons.[12]

Let us not annul the blessed doctrine of divine sovereignty with our apathy, slackness, and deadness of soul. Preach as though all depends on you, and leave the results to God.

A further warning is added from Baxter's writings:

If you say that the work is God's, and he may do it by the weakest means, I answer, It is true, he may do so; but yet his ordinary way is to work by means, and to make not only the matter that is preached, but also the manner of preaching instrumental to the work.[13]

That is balanced preaching!

An Urgent Need for Urgency

The matter of urgency is sorely lacking today. For some reason, so many of us have lost it or never had it to begin with. If we are ever to move the hearts of people, we must impress upon them the urgent matters of life in an urgent manner of speaking. If this will not move them, perhaps nothing will—but we will have done our best effort!

6

Preach with Brokenness

I am well content with weaknesses, with insults, with distresses, with persecutions, with difficulties, for Christ's sake; for when I am weak, then I am strong.

—2 Corinthians 12:10

A pastor and his wife went to listen to a promising young preacher one day. The pastor turned to his wife and said, "He is a good preacher." "Yes," she answered, "but he will be better once he has suffered for a while!" Great preachers are forged in the furnace of affliction.

It is an inconvertible truth that afflictions, trials, and testings are a prerequisite to truly great passionate preaching. If preaching is God's Word through a man, that man must be made a fit vessel for the dispensing of that truth! Such preparation comes by means of trials. Alexander Maclaren said, "It takes a crucified man to preach a crucified Savior."[1] God does not mightily use a preacher until he has made him human, until he becomes like his Master, "a man of sorrows and acquainted with grief" (Isa. 53:3). A flower must be crushed to release its fragrance, the vessel must be broken to pour forth its anointing perfume, and so the human vial must also be crushed and broken so that the sweet words of grace can pour forth to be a savor of life and of death!

> ### *"Great preachers are forged in the furnace of affliction."*

God's flock is a bruised and battered lot. Joseph Parker said, "If you preach to hurting hearts, you will never want for a congregation; there is one in every pew."[2] The only catch is that you need to be a broken man to be capable of preaching to broken hearts. Vines rightly asserts,

> When our hearts are broken, we learn how to preach to others who have broken hearts. Preaching is to break hard hearts and heal broken hearts. That is most effectively done when the preacher has been through his own valley.[3]

Brokenness is a requirement for strong, vigorous, and passionate preaching. A moist eye and an aching heart provide rare eloquence to preaching!

Although I believe seminary training is an indispensable element
in the preparation of the man of God to occupy the sacred pulpit, I
also agree that it comes up short in thoroughly preparing a man for
effective ministry. Seminaries are neither prepared to baptize the pulpit
in the waters of affliction, nor can they make the student drink from
the cup of suffering (Mark 10:38–39). There remains a class taught by
the Master Himself, where the Lord leads the man of God through
the deep valley of affliction until he emerges a broken, yielded servant of God. Seminarians think that a little Hebrew mixed with a little
Greek, seasoned with theology and Bible, and served on a homiletical
plate constitute preaching and comprise the elements of a preacher.
Wrong! *Seminary trains the mind, but suffering trains the soul.*

The Bible speaks forthrightly and positively about the place that
trials have in the life of the believer, and how much more in the life
of the preacher:

> *Blessed are you when men revile you, and persecute you, and
> say all kinds of evil against you falsely, on account of Me.
> Rejoice, and be glad, for your reward in heaven is great, for
> so they persecuted the prophets who were before you.*
> —Matthew 5:11–12

> *So they went on their way from the presence of the Council,
> rejoicing that they had been considered worthy to suffer
> shame for His name.*
> —Acts 5:41

> *And not only this, but we also exult in our tribulations, know-
> ing that tribulation brings about perseverance; and persever-
> ance, proven character; and proven character, hope; and hope
> does not disappoint, because the love of God has been poured
> out within our hearts through the Holy Spirit who was given
> to us.*
> —Romans 5:3–5

> *For to you it has been granted for Christ's sake, not only to*

believe in Him, but also to suffer for His sake, experiencing the same conflict which you saw in me, and now hear to be in me.

—Philippians 1:29–30

For those whom the Lord loves He disciplines, and He scourges every son whom He receives. . . . All discipline for the moment seems not to be joyful, but sorrowful; yet to those who have been trained by it, afterwards it yields the peaceful fruit of righteousness.

—Hebrews 12:6, 11

Consider it all joy, my brethren, when you encounter various trials, knowing that the testing of your faith produces endurance. And let endurance have its perfect result, that you may be perfect and complete, lacking in nothing. . . . Blessed is the man who perseveres under trial; for once he has been approved, he will receive the crown of life, which the Lord has promised to those who love Him.

—James 1:2–4, 12

In this you greatly rejoice, even though now for a little while, if necessary, you have been distressed by various trials, that the proof of your faith, being more precious than gold which is perishable, even though tested by fire, may be found to result in praise and glory and honor at the revelation of Jesus Christ.

—1 Peter 1:6–7

In short, trials are the refining fire of the Lord to purify His servants and fit them for effective service.

The Effects of Brokenness

The Lord must burn the dross out of His ministers. Every impurity that would hinder the Word of God must be wiped clean from

His chosen vessels. Much of a man's impurity is wrapped up in *self:* self-righteousness, self-sufficiency, selfishness, and even self-worship. Like gold in a crucible, so the heart of the preacher must be so purified that God looking in sees His face and nothing of man. God breaks a man who is full of himself; then he is useful to God.

The Effects of Brokenness

- ▶ Humility
- ▶ Faith and dependence
- ▶ Compassion and love
- ▶ Realism
- ▶ Sobriety
- ▶ Righteous indignation
- ▶ Boldness

1. *Humility.* A broken man is a humble man. Pride is opposed to obedience. Pride is the twin of self-righteousness. Pride is no one's servant, and no one's caretaker. Hence, God has no use for a proud man. In fact, such men are in danger of becoming conceited and of falling into the condemnation incurred by the devil (cf. 1 Tim. 3:6). Scripture is unequivocal: "God is opposed to the proud, but gives grace to the humble" (James 4:6).

God's greatest servants were broken by Him of their pride before they were used mightily. Moses sought to liberate Israel by his own strength and power, only to meet rejection by his people and banishment from Egypt. He lived an obscure shepherd's life in the wilderness. What a contrast with the glories of Egypt! What a time of refining by the desolation of the desert! Yet after forty years, God could say of Moses, "Now the man Moses was very humble, more than any man who was on the face of the earth" (Num. 12:3). As the staff was in the hand of Moses to turn wherever he would dictate, so was Moses in the hand of God. Few, if any mortals, have attained such a place in the history of redemption!

Then there is Job! Who would ever have thought that there were any impurities in Job? Even Job argued with God over his treatment, vacillating between despair and disapproval because he thought himself clean. Yet we know that even this great man had room for improvement. He, too, was plagued with pride. So God broke him through disaster, death, disease, derision, and desertion! He was left alone on an ash heap to ponder the great mystery of the universe: Why do the righteous suffer? Then he found the answer: Because no one is righteous enough! In the end, Job repents in dust and ashes, a broken man.

The New Testament counterpart is the apostle Peter. We love to point out his personal flaws: impetuous, loud, and boisterous! Yet he was the most loyal and believing of the disciples. Remember, he alone of the disciples walked on water. But Peter, too, needed to be broken of his pride. He, too, jostled with the other disciples over who was the greatest. On the darkest night they displayed their darkest side: pride (cf. Luke 22:23–24). Yet Jesus foretold a time of purifying for Peter followed by greater usefulness to Christ. Although Peter objected, the words of Christ prevailed, and Peter was purged of his self-glorying (cf. Luke 22:31–34). Now he was a humble vessel, sanctified and useful to the Master! Now he was a "fellow elder," not the chief elder or pope! He was a broken man.

A pulpit in the hands of an unbroken man becomes a throne from which he demands worship for his artistry. But to a broken man, the pulpit is a yoke that straps him to his fellow man to carry him along the road of life. The pulpit is then not a weapon but a tool to bring encouragement and to comfort.

> *"To a broken man the pulpit is a yoke that straps him to his fellow man to carry him along the road of life."*

Are you in the midst of trials? Perhaps God is endeavoring to humble you, to make you more of a servant, that you may be trusted with more of His vineyard!

2. *Faith.* The chief goal of preaching is to turn people's hearts to God, to create faith, living faith in God. That's how the writer to the

Hebrews describes the leader: "Remember those who led you, who spoke the word of God to you; and considering the outcome of their way of life, imitate their faith" (Heb. 13:7). Paul admonishes Timothy to be an "example of those who believe" (1 Tim. 4:12).

The preacher must himself be a man of faith not only to point the way to God but also to show by his life that he, too, lives in constant dependence upon God. Self-reliance and self-sufficiency is *faithlessness*. The average person in the pew knows he cannot do without God. But does the man in the pulpit know it? Does he live a life of dependence upon God?

The apostle Paul, in his second letter to the Corinthians, tells how God broke him and taught him utter dependence upon God. We read between the lines that Paul's self-reliance was still a hindrance to ministry. The Lord gave Paul a "thorn in the flesh, a messenger from Satan," to keep him from exalting himself. God chose not to hear Paul's prayer for deliverance but rather used this affliction to teach Paul dependence on God (2 Cor. 12:7–8). Note how Paul glories in his brokenness:

> *And he said to me, " My grace is sufficient for you, for power is perfected in weakness." Most gladly, therefore, I will rather boast about my weaknesses, that the power of Christ may dwell in me. Therefore I am well content with weaknesses, with insults, with distresses, with persecutions, with difficulties, for Christ's sake; for when I am weak, then I am strong.*
> —2 Corinthians 12:9–10

A broken man—instead of being a weak man—is made stronger because his trust is in the Lord. He knows God and so can make Him known.

3. *Compassion.* Someone defined compassion as "your pain in my heart." Such pain is better felt when we go through the same trials. I will not repeat the matters discussed in the chapter on compassion, but I want to emphasize here that compassion comes by means of brokenness. We can do a better job of preaching to heal the hurts of others when we have experienced the healing hand of God upon our own hurts. This is what qualified Paul to be a healer of souls:

Blessed be the God and Father of our Lord Jesus Christ, the Father of mercies and God of all comfort; who comforts us in all our affliction so that we may be able to comfort those who are in any affliction with the comfort with which we ourselves are comforted by God.

—2 Corinthians 1:3–4

We can attest to the goodness and mercy of God when we have a firsthand experience.

For some reason, God's people will be more inclined to listen to us when we can say, "I have been through the same tough times." They know we can honestly feel their pain. A sage said, "We ought never criticize a man until we have walked in his shoes for a mile!" There is wisdom here. God makes us able ministers and preachers by forcing us to walk in the shoes of our people for a mile or two.

The major difference in my preaching today over that of my early years is that now I preach as one of them. Back then I preached sermons *to* them. I was more concerned about my own involvement in the text, the mode of delivery, and the visible and immediate response to the message. Now the seasons of life have left me scarred and wounded. My preaching today is deeply concerned about how I can bring healing to a hurting congregation. I have learned to sympathize with them.

> **bro•ken•ness** *n.* weakened in strength, spirit; reduced to submission; overwhelmed with sorrow.[4]

4. *Realism.* We have been accused of being "other worldly," not that we are heavenly, but that we seem to come from another planet or with an obscure perspective. We preach about things that people do not experience, nor will ever experience. It seems as though some of us live in another century, others in another decade, and still others in another country.

It is possible to read the Bible with rose-tinted glasses, where we look for the ideal setting. We preach as though all of the great men and women of the Bible were perfect. When we preach about Bible characters, we see only their virtues and never their failures. We imply that the New Testament churches were ideal and that ours are so far away from their example. But if we were honest, our churches *are* just like them—imperfect, sometimes unattractive, and even embarrassing. Yet somehow we are unable to present the real picture to our people.

Seminarians and young preachers are idealists. They tend to see the world as it should be and not as it really is. This idealism governs the way they act and address issues in life. A single man speaks of the ideal marriage. The childless couple speaks of the ideal family. The young father speaks of the ideal teenager, and so on. This idealism is neither realistic nor fair! It is a burden that no one should be made to bear! The fact is that the world is fallen and full of imperfections. Life is tainted! We strive only to make the most of it and, at times, improve it.

Brokenness has the effect of teaching us to live in a real world, full of hurts and disappointments, failures and fears, stains and blemishes. "Get real!" is what God tells us. "Remove the rose-colored glasses! See the world for what it really is! *Then* address this messed-up world!"

We need honesty here. Preachers sometimes do not live in the same world as their congregations. Some do not live in the same community. They do not even send their children to public schools. They do not have the same pay scale (they often make more money), and they do not work the same workweek (some work fewer hours than the average household)! From their ivory towers, they lay down principles for living that have never been tested in real life.

Yet the school of life is a great equalizer. Life has a way of giving all of us a reality check. All of the hard realities come crashing in and burst our ideal bubble. We learn that churches do not grow overnight (if they grow at all), that our preaching does not compare to MacArthur's or Swindoll's, that the people of God can be cruel and do not grow out of it, that our marriage does have its warps, that our children do disobey, and that ministry can be a real burden. Welcome to the real world! Now God is able to use you. Now your preaching has an air of authenticity. "This man lives in my world," your congregation will say of you!

We as preachers will learn that God's Word and the principles taught in it do work in a less than perfect world. Perfection is not a prerequisite for happiness. God can bring joy to a widow or unmarried single. God does give grace to a sickness when He denies the cry for healing. Money is not the answer to all things. Routines and dry times are part of the great fabric of life. So we learn to enjoy the refreshing breaks, however few they are! The book of Ecclesiastes was written by a preacher for preachers. Vanity is part of the real world, but it is not the end. When our feet are placed solidly on the ground, we can begin to live and begin to preach passionately.

"God's school of hard knocks teaches us to focus on those things which really matter in life."

---

5. *Sobriety.* Close to realism is what I would call "sobriety." Just as trials burst the bubbles of idealism, afflictions have a way of removing the chaff in our lives. God's school of hard knocks teaches us to focus on those things that really matter in life. *Perspective* or *focus* may be the words. I like the word *sober*—one who is not intoxicated with the foolish things of this world. God appeals to us often to live *sober* lives:

> *Be sober in all things.*
> —2 Timothy 4:5

> *For the grace of God has appeared . . . instructing us to deny ungodliness and worldly desires and to live sensibly.*
> —Titus 2:11–12

> *Therefore, gird your minds for action, keep sober in spirit.*
> —1 Peter 1:13

The end of all things is at hand; therefore, be of sound judgment and sober spirit for the purpose of prayer.
—1 Peter 4:7

Be of sober spirit, be on the alert. Your adversary, the devil, prowls about like a roaring lion, seeking someone to devour.
—1 Peter 5:8

When God sifts you like wheat, when He crushes you beneath the millstone of life, the chaff becomes visible and easily separated. It is amazing how much excess baggage we collect in life, much of which is simply just chaff. When the early pioneers made the long trek west over the Oregon trail, they soon learned to distinguish between what was essential for life and what was not. The trail was soon littered with the "chaff" of life. The difficulties in our journey teach us the same!

The church that split over the color of the carpet in the sanctuary is proverbial. That church was split by men who never knew the agony of building a church, nor of the heartbreak of picking up the pieces of a church split. To a broken man, the color of the carpet is a nonessential. In fact, the carpet itself is immaterial to the welfare of the flock. But it takes a broken man to see through the chaff of life.

Our preaching can be full of this stuff, the chaff of life. It has no eternal significance—it will not matter even three months from now. Powerful preaching deals with eternal truths, the real "stuff" of life. We desperately need more sobriety in our living and thus in our preaching. A preacher who lives soberly will preach soberly, but only a man who has been broken will live soberly.

Let me add a word here. Soberness is not the same as *melancholy*. Life has its lighter side. Laughter—as well as tears—is a gift from God. Joy, laughter, and even humor has its place in the pulpit. The pilgrim's journey to the Celestial City should avoid By-path Meadow and Vanity Fair, but song and laughter should also accompany it. Soberness and seriousness is not the same as sadness and a melancholy spirit.

6. *Righteous indignation.* A truly broken preacher is a fiery preacher. The walk through the valley of death has impressed upon

him the real and awful consequences of sin. When a man has experienced the ravages of it either in his own life or in the lives of others, he can no longer be a silent bystander. He must cry out against sin. A preacher broken by such effects of sin is filled with righteous indignation. There is a lion-like demeanor about him in declaring the oracles of God.

Sin and the world are no friends to us, and we should not seek their friendship. Sin should provoke us to righteous wrath, and it does when it is rightly assessed. Why is there so little indignation in our pulpits? Why is there little denunciation of ungodliness? Why is there all this psychological babble about the kind treatment of evil? Could it be because these idle soothsayers have no knowledge of sin or of the Savior's cross?

To see Christ is to see one filled with righteous indignation against hardness of heart (Mark 3:5) and hypocrisy (Matt. 23:1ff.). Peter was indignant against Simon's lust for power (Acts 8:20–23) and Paul against legalism (Gal. 6:11–17; Phil. 3:17–19). The destructive and devastating nature of sin prompted a heated response. Should we not do the same?

An extramarital affair leaves divorce or destruction in its wake. Fornication yields an unwed mother and an unwanted child. Drinking and drugs leave an impoverished home, an abused spouse, and a deranged abuser. Social injustices, like bigotry and racism, breed anger and segregation. Murder, rape, brutality—all are great evils permeating our culture. Economic oppression by greedy businesses or thieves in the workplace is a cancerous sore affecting many of us. Violation of basic human rights is everyone's business. When these affect you, they become your business, and you are forced to speak out against them.

7. *Holy boldness.* Another effect of brokenness is *holy boldness.* The wife of a dear friend of mine contracted a deadly cancer, which—needless to say—had a great effect upon her life. One effect is that it made her bold! She was afraid of nothing and no one. When death is sure, it loses its ferociousness. It is not feared!

The same thing happens to a preacher. A life lived on the edge results in a life lived without fear of consequences. We see that in

America today. The pulpits are occupied by men who were converted out of a life of sin and despair. Some of these were the street people of the 60s. Few things frightened them. Neither politics nor poverty nor pain—nor even death—is a threat to them. They have been inoculated against the fear of those things.

Paul's frequent brushes with death made him a fearless preacher (cf. 2 Cor. 11:23–28). His motto was, "For me, to live is Christ, and to die is gain" (Phil. 1:21). The apostle was truly a crucified man able to speak about a crucified Savior. The apostle Peter was no different (cf. 2 Peter 1:13–14).

The man who knows poverty will not fear poverty. The man who knows pain will not fear pain. The man who knows loneliness will not fear loss or recognition. If a man has had the death dew on his brow, he will not fear man or devils! Martin Luther, the great Reformer, knew all of these things, and God used him to lead a mighty reformation against the Roman Catholic Church.

Are you fearful? Does the Lord have you living on the edge? Is your life paralyzed with anxiety and doubt? Are you fearful of your congregation? God is forging a man of steel. Once you pass through the fire, you will be less fearful and more filled with holy boldness. Passionate preaching knows only one fear, the fear of God!

Are You Willing to Suffer?

The truth is, none of us likes the idea of being broken. We dread the thought that God must take us through an hour of testing to form a preacher. It would be nice to be able to preach great sermons that bring great good without going through great affliction. But this is not possible! If we would live deeply and preach deeply, we must suffer deeply. So remember: you may be a good preacher now, but you will be a better one once you have suffered a while!

7

Preach with the Whole Being

When he had given him permission, Paul, standing on the stairs, motioned to the people with his hand; and when there was a great hush, he spoke to them in the Hebrew dialect.

—Acts 21:40

P reaching today is mainly verbal. Yet biblical preaching as we see in the preaching of Christ and Paul is more than just verbal. Indeed, passionate biblical preaching entails the lively exercise of our entire body. Effective communication can be accomplished only when we use our entire body to get our message across.

Our whole discussion of passion in preaching has been and continues to be on delivering the message. Delivery is crucial to effective, biblical preaching. In fact, all rests on delivery:

> The delivery of the sermon is the most dynamic moment of the preaching experience. In that moment all sermon preparation is brought to fruition or frustration. If the sermon is delivered effectively, the preacher, in grateful joy, forgets the hours of toil in preparation. But if the sermon fails, all the labor and study will seem like a heavy and useless burden. The Gospel is a proclaimed gospel. Thus a sermon is never a sermon until it is delivered. A minister is never a preacher until the message is communicated to others.[1]

We need to pay very close attention to this matter of delivery. How we say what we have to say is crucial, and how we say it involves more than words—*it involves our bodies.* Our whole being must be involved in the communicative process. Richard Baxter lays this stinging charge to all of us:

> With the most of our hearers, the very pronunciation and tone of speech is a great point. The best matter will scarcely move them, if it be not movingly delivered. . . . A sermon full of mere words, how neatly soever it be composed, while it wants the light of evidence, and the life of zeal, is but an image or a well-dressed carcass.[2]

"Passionate biblical preaching entails the lively exercise of the entire body."

Dead men do not awaken the dead. It must be visually as well as audibly evident that we are alive. But if we are immovable stone statues petrified behind our pulpits, how can we arouse the dead? Preaching must be lively, and lively preaching means a free, natural, and expressive use of our bodies—eyes, limbs, and all!

Use your entire body, preacher! Effective communication requires it! Use verbal language, but back it up with body language. In fact, just persuade yourself that one must accompany the other. Fasol asserts,

> Nonverbal communication, more popularly referred to as *body language,* includes these factors: personal appearance, perceptions gained by the congregation in their first impressions of the speaker, walking to the pulpit or lectern, eye contact, facial expressions, posture, and gestures. These visible communication signals either support or hinder the message being expressed through language and voice. Body language communicates a message without saying a word. In preaching, body language should support content.[3]

My aim in this section is to move you to learn to preach with your whole body. Passionate preaching demands it. As a preacher, you must learn to use the body as an aid to communication. This is not something taught in speech courses or in homiletics classes, probably because normal human communication naturally involves the use of our bodies. Christian preaching creates an artificial arena where the preacher is removed from the audience, where the pulpit acts as a barrier and a straitjacket, and where the act of preaching is more like an address or lecture. The body is not used effectively to communicate. We need to free up ourselves to preach effectively. We need to free up our hearts, our eyes, our hands, and our torsos to aid in the communication of the words we have prepared!

> **ges•ture** *n.* a movement or position of the hand, arm, body, head, or face that is expressive of an idea, opinion, or emotion.[4]

If we are to preach with passion, we must put the whole self into our preaching. After we have loaded the cannon for firing, we must ram ourselves into the barrel and fire away. Vines writes, "The preacher not only delivers his sermon; he also delivers himself." Again he states, "In one sense of the word we might say that sermon delivery is not so much the art of the preacher's delivering a sermon as it is of the preacher's delivering himself."[5]

Yet Stephen Olford offers a much-needed caution:

> The appearance and appeal should be governed by the truth and the Spirit. Gestures, facial expressions, and the whole ethos of the preacher ought to be Christ-like and "message-like." The body language and facial expressions of the preacher should be reflective and expressive of the message itself. An incarnational message should come through the preacher with the honest appearance of personal ownership, and this should translate into gestures and expressions in keeping with the message and, of course, the personality of the preacher.[6]

In short, be honest and be yourself. This point may need some explanation since many beginning preachers are introverted by nature, or are reserved due to the need for propriety in the pulpit, or subdued for fear of "doing the Spirit's work." Hence, for most of us, using our entire body in preaching will seem very awkward. The remedy for this is twofold. First, understand the importance of body language to effective preaching, and choose to err on the side of effective delivery. Second, videotape a session in which you think you are being unnatural as you use your body to preach. You will see that not only are you not acting like a clown, but that your body language accentuates your content! Practice preaching this way until it feels comfortable. This will become your pulpit style, and it will honestly be you. You will no longer feel like an actor, but will actually feel quite comfortable.

Let me address five areas of importance concerning body language, or communication with the whole being.

Areas of Importance when Communicating with the Whole Being

- ▶ The heart
- ▶ The eyes
- ▶ The voice
- ▶ The arms
- ▶ The torso

Preach with Passion in Your Heart

The preacher must allow himself to feel deeply about his subject and about his audience. As a rule, we like to be in firm control of our emotions; we would never want to "lose it" in the pulpit. Some people would consider it "bad preaching" if somehow the preacher was "beside himself" as he preached, if his emotions ran ahead of his reasoning, or if his emotions arrested his speaking so that he was unable to continue his oration. But is this not the case with all true human endeavors that call upon the total exertion of the human soul? Is it not the case with great athletes who triumph after total exertion? Do they not burst into tears or unrestrained celebration? Is this not the case with doctors, firefighters, rescue workers, and the like? Their adrenaline level far exceeds what the normal levels would dictate. Why? Because the occasion calls for total involvement, not just of the mind, but also of the whole body.

In this great task of preaching the Word of God, does it not also demand that we pour out ourselves before the Lord? Does not a lost soul demand our all in its rescue? Consider our Lord Jesus Christ in His great triumphal entry and how He was overcome by emotion to the point of weeping loudly when He foresaw the destruction of His beloved city, Jerusalem (Luke 19:41–44). His was a passionate life! Christ did not just preach passionately; He lived passionately.

Hence, let the great truths lay hold of your heart. Let your heart be lifted and carried along by your care and concern for the souls of people. Let us be as the apostle Paul, who also lived passionately. Notice how he expressed his emotion to the churches at Thessalonica and Corinth:

*Having thus a fond affection for you, we were well pleased
to impart to you not only the gospel but also our own lives,
because you had become very dear to us.*
                                        —1 Thessalonians 2:8

I will most gladly spend and be expended for your souls.
                                        —2 Corinthians 12:15

Our bodies often do not correspond to our message, I fear, because
our emotions are harnessed more to the will than to the heart. We
deny our hearts the right to feel the truth we preach, and yet the heart
is the control station for the rest of the body. The body will do as the
heart feels. Contrast the body language of the tax collector with the
Pharisee in Luke 18:9–14. Each man's body followed the state of the
heart. The Pharisee's words and the position of his body confirmed
his proud heart. His eyes no doubt were shut, for he was praying to
himself. On the other hand, the tax collector had his eyes down, his
body scarcely inside the temple, and his fist afflicting blows to a deeply
wounded heart! His body language corresponded with his words. In
fact, notice how much the Lord's description of their body language
adds to the color and contrast of the parable!

Preach with Passion in Your Eyes and Face

Dr. Robinson states, "As important as grooming and movement are
to a speaker, eye contact probably ranks as the most effective single
means of nonverbal communication at his disposal. Eyes communicate."[7] Jerry Vines writes, "The eyes are the most eloquent part of the
body."[8] Most preachers think the primary use of the eyes is to read
their notes or manuscripts. That is secondary. The primary use of the
eyes is to make contact with the listener. Through your eyes, you allow the listeners to look into your soul, even as you look into theirs.
The eyes also most fully reveal the state of your emotions. Anger,
sadness, joy, gladness, and love—all these come most clearly through
your eyes.

> *"The preacher's facial expressions can affirm and confirm a truth in ways that even argumentation and illustration cannot."*

The face is like the eyes. Your face affirms or contradicts your message. Your face also wins or loses the confidence of the audience. "The preacher's facial expressions," states Olford, "can affirm and confirm a truth in ways that even argumentation and illustration cannot."[9] Preachers have not paid enough attention to the role that our facial expressions have on our sermons. Consider the following.

If your eye contact is the most vital use of the body, facial expression is the most neglected physical action. The face has tremendous potential for expressing the changing moods and meanings of the sermon. But many never adequately permit the face to express their inner feelings.[10]

Methods of Sermon Delivery

- ▶ Reading
- ▶ Recitation
- ▶ Impromptu
- ▶ Extemporaneous

Here is a good place to discuss the different methods of sermon delivery: reading, recitation from memory, impromptu, and extemporaneous. If the eyes and face play such a vital role in the act of communication, then it is only logical to conclude that the most effective method of delivery is that which frees up the eyes and face to become part of the sermon, to assist in the delivery. *Reading* is most logically at the bottom of the list since it ties the eyes and face to the manuscript. There are very few examples of effective communicators who are also readers. *Recitation* is much too strenuous to be of any use to a contemporary evangelical preacher who preaches two or three times a week. The *impromptu method*, that of preaching without notes or planned preparation, is excellent but beyond the grasp of all but the most gifted and prepared minds, like Spurgeon's!

The *extemporaneous method* is that which studies a subject thoroughly and then seeks to present the material without the aid of a written manuscript and with as few notes as possible. This method frees the eyes to focus on the audience instead of being glued to a manuscript.

So many things are taking place while one is preaching. The audience is reacting to us, sizing us up, deciding if they can trust us, and determining if they like us. In addition, throughout the sermon the audience is trying to follow the various movements of the message. We can lose them right at the start or at any juncture along the way. We need to learn to develop *audience awareness*, namely, to learn to read our audience to see whether they are with us and understanding what we are teaching, or whether they are agreeing or disagreeing with us.

It is extremely tragic when a preacher is unaware of how his audience is responding to his message. Yet so many preachers drone on even when the audience gets off at the last stop, and they are totally unaware of it. More intent on giving information, they miss the whole point of preaching. When the audience stops listening, the preacher should stop preaching. You can only know this if your countenance is free to engage theirs.

The eyes communicate. Use them! Let them be part of your arsenal to communicate the truth of God. Our Lord did! Mark tells us that our Lord revealed through His eyes His anger (Mark 4:5) as well as His love (Mark 10:21). His passion came through His countenance! His eyes spoke what was in His heart, and the disciples read Him clearly.

Preach with Passion in Your Voice

Preaching with the whole being includes the natural use of the voice in expressing the emotions contained in our message. Passion is expressed in our voices through tone, rate, volume, and projection. Yet how often have we been accused of being monotonous! We speak dispassionately about passionate issues. What a contradiction! "Monotony," says Broadus, "is utterly destructive of eloquence."[11] Spurgeon had this to say about monotonous preaching:

> It is a most barbarous thing to inflict upon the tympanum of a poor fellow-creature's ear the anguish of being bored and gimbleted with the same sound for half an hour. What swifter mode of rendering the mind idiotic or lunatic could be conceived than the perpetual droning of a beetle, or buzzing of a blue-bottle, in the organ of hearing? What dispensation have you by which you are to be tolerated in such cruelty to the helpless victims who sit under your drum-drum ministrations? Kind nature frequently spares the drone's unhappy victims the full effect of his tortures by steeping them in sweet repose. This, however, you do not desire; then speak with a varied voice. How few ministers remember that monotony causes sleep.[12]

Get the point?

Passionate preaching has great variety, simply because the emotions are excited and so rise and fall with the sentiments of the preacher. Variety includes the rate with which one speaks, sometimes rapidly as when excited, other times slow and ponderous as when deliberating or making proper use of the pause. The voice will be loud one moment and then as soft and still as the summer breeze. As variety is the spice of life, so variety in the voice calls for attention. Variety is gained when we take care to have a real and marked variety in our sentiments, and then simply speaking each particular sentiment in the most natural manner.[13] Variety is achieved when,

> The preacher speaks naturally in such an animated way as to reflect the changing moods and meanings of the sermon. Such animated and natural speech is characteristic of conversational delivery. Conversational delivery does not mean subdued or

"soft" speech. Rather, it means that the speaker, in the heightened force of platform delivery, is warm, personal, alive, and is speaking as if in personal conversation. Such delivery, flexible in every phase of vocal production, is forceful. The audience *must* listen![14]

Preach with Passion in Your Arms

The use of the arms and hands in preaching we call "gestures." In normal speech, gestures come naturally without forethought and are of great benefit in communication. Preaching *should* make use of gestures, and passionate preaching *will* make full and effective use of gestures. We often tend to minimize the importance that the arms and hands play in communication. Broadus states,

> Certainly the hands and arms in gesture are of unequaled importance. . . . As to the hands, without which delivery would be mutilated and feeble, it can scarcely be said how many movements they have, when they almost equal the number of words. For other parts of the person help the speaker; these . . . speak for themselves.[15]

You would not want to preach without the useful employment of your hands and arms. They are your allies. They speak for you what words alone cannot adequately convey. Life has taught us to draw pictures with our hands, and these nursery instructions carry over into adult reasonings.

For gestures to be effective, they must be natural, "impulsive reflections on the speaker's feelings."[16] Gestures also must be appropriate. Vines states,

> You should suit the action to the word and the word to the action. In a sense, the preacher gives two speeches at the same time: that which his listeners hear and that which they see. To be the most effective, the preacher should mold the two speeches to form one communicative process.[17]

We should not be timid in the use of our hands and arms in preaching. It is better to err on the side of being too expressive than to imply by our lack of expression that what we are saying is not vitally important. So raise the hand, clench the fist, point the finger, extend the arms, wave off the bad, and direct the way to heaven with your arms. All these and more should accompany your verbal communication.

"It is better to err on the side of being too expressive than to imply by lack of expression that what you are saying is not important."

Remember that the larger the audience, the more your gestures must be emphasized. Enlarge the example so that those in the farthest seats read both sermons. Also, there may be little need to practice our gestures if we allow ourselves the freedom to speak as we feel. Yet, a view of ourselves on videotape might alert us to the use or nonuse of gestures. Then for some time we need to think of gesturing as we preach. I like what Broadus adds:

> In general, one should never regress a movement to which he is inclined because he is afraid it may not be graceful. After all, life and power are far more important than grace; and, in fact, timid self-regression destroys grace itself.[18]

Preach with Passion in Your Body

The preacher who desires to be an effective communicator must use his whole body as he preaches. Yet most of us are encased in a pulpit that shields us from view; this would hamper us even if we wanted to use our bodies to communicate. No wonder that great pulpiteers of the past and present chose to do away with large pulpits, electing to have simple lecterns instead. They want to have full use of the body when they preach!

The importance of using the body to communicate is vital for all preachers to understand, especially if we want to be effective communicators.[19] You cannot stand behind the pulpit without giving conscious, careful thought to appearance, posture, and proper movement of the body in delivery. Modern technology has given us the freedom to move about as we preach. This surely enhances communication when used properly. The whole body is free to be used to express our thoughts. What can be more liberating and more effective? Vines writes, "Good bodily movement is a positive factor in holding attention. . . . The preacher who stands lifelessly and listlessly in the pulpit almost guarantees that his audience will be disinterested."[20]

Be Free!

I have made a case for the use of the whole body in preaching. This is the normal way we converse with one another. Should we not do the same as we converse with our people about spiritual things? In my plea to have you preach with passion, let me reiterate that if you unlock the channels inhibiting free expression of thought through your bodily members, you will become a more expressive preacher. You *will* communicate with passion.

8

Preach with Imagination

Therefore every one who hears these words of Mine, and acts upon them, may be compared to a wise man, who built his house upon the rock.

—Matthew 7:24

Passionate preaching is by its very nature imaginative, colorful, stirring preaching because it proceeds from the heart, the seat of emotions. Head preaching is abstract; heart preaching is concrete. Head preaching is cold and lifeless; heart preaching is vivid and emotional.

This chapter will focus on the unique aspect of preaching that deals with the use of imagination. By imagination, I mean the use of the rhetorical tools available to us to make our thoughts as true to life as possible, as concrete as possible, and as colorful and as clear as words can make truth. Calvin Miller reminds us that there are at least two ways to say something: "the more powerful and the less powerful."[1] We choose one or the other. Obviously, if we intend to preach passionately, we must choose the more powerful way to express our message.

> **im•ag•i•na•tion** n. the action or faculty of forming mental images or concepts of what is not actually present to the senses; creative talent or ability.[2]

Unfortunately, many of us have unconsciously chosen the other form, the less powerful way of communication. By defaulting on the need for imagination in our preaching, we preach lifeless words, colorless characters, and bland bundles of exegetical insights. The result? A powerless sermon. Perhaps some among us decry the use of imagination in preaching and purposefully set out to make their sermons abstract, colorless, and unemotional. Such sermons are dull and unimpressive to the average listener. Gardner C. Tayler, considered the "dean" of Black preachers in America, said,

> The mode of expression today has become more metallic. . . . I mean a certain flat, pedestrian language that does not fire the imagination. It is not gripping. Preaching may be confrontational sometimes, certainly exhortatory, but it should have

an added sense of the majesty of life, the glory of its possibilities, and the greatness and glory of God. It's saying something, but it's saying something in a glorious way.[3]

Do we say something in a glorious way? Examine the last sermon you preached. Did you endeavor to frame your thoughts *purposely* to say things powerfully, to add a dimension of grandeur to your exposition?

As we have noted before, biblical preaching is not merely the communicating of biblical content. It goes beyond that to include the explanation and application of those truths.[4] The end of all preaching is to persuade the hearer to respond favorably, volitionally, and wholeheartedly to the truth. *All preaching is purposeful preaching.* To achieve this end, affecting the emotions is a must. Action cannot be expected if the emotions are left untouched. Dr. John MacArthur concurs:

> Emotions are important. They were given to us by God, and they often move the will. People do not usually make decisions in an emotional vacuum. I do want to stir people's emotions when I preach, because truth that warms the heart can move the will. . . It should be our goal to encourage the proper components in worship. The hymns and special music, as well as pastoral prayer and sermon, must articulate truth. Yet they should also stir the emotions and activate the will.[5]

To be passionate, expository preaching must use imagination to stir the emotions to bring about the submission of the will.

"The listener does not have the luxury of rereading the paragraph. He hears the truth but once, and if it is not outfitted with the proper means of impacting his heart, he gets no second chance."

The craft of sermon preparation should include a serious discussion of this important aspect of preaching. In the delivery of the sermon, how we say something is as important as what we say, and more so because the listener does not have the luxury of rereading the paragraph. He hears the truth but once, and if the truth is not outfitted with the proper means of impacting his heart and soul, he gets no second chance. Let us not minimize this. Remember, "truth made concrete will find a way past many a door when abstractions knock in vain."[6] Again,

> Imagination lends a statement emotional and moral significance, makes it mean something to the listener, turns truth into power, adds depth and insight to knowledge, engages feeling and memory, sympathy and indignation, interest and response, on behalf of what is said.[7]

To help us preach with imagination, I will first show how the Bible itself is an imaginative book, that the biblical writers and preachers made use of imaginative tools to communicate. Then I will explore the specific tools available to us to help us construct more powerful sermons. Finally, I will add several steps that we must take to develop imagination in our preaching.

Imagination in the Scriptures

When we listen to ourselves preach, and then read how the Bible addresses truth and reveals God's will, and how the prophets and preachers of old spoke and taught, we wonder sometimes where and how we got off track. The Bible is an imaginative book. The people who wrote and spoke were almost all imaginative communicators. They spoke in stories, in pictures, in metaphors, in parables, and in events in their daily lives. Truth came packaged in human garb. "To preach biblically," argues Warren Wiersbe, "means much more than to preach the truth of the Bible accurately. It also means to present that truth the way the biblical writers and speakers presented it, and that means addressing the imagination."[8]

Preaching is a very personal matter, and so not everyone takes such advice readily or willingly. Yet we can see over and over again that the biblical writers and preachers used imagination under divine sanction. White argues rather convincingly:

> It is to be feared that none of this will change the habit of the man who is convinced that souls are saved by right doctrine, and that the plain statement of the truth is all that is required of the preacher. Yet even such a preacher, prosy, unimaginative, unsympathetic, abstract, may admit that the Master preacher may have something to teach him. None of this argumentation in favour of developing the discipline of the imagination for pulpit use is necessary for anyone who ever really listened to Jesus.[9]

The Scriptures present truth in story, in poetry, in prose, and even through visions and apocalyptic literature. Each of these genres is full of imaginative devices that drive God's Word toward its mark. If, as Peter writes, "men moved by the Holy Spirit spoke from God" (2 Peter 1:21), then God chose to use imaginative communication to speak to mankind. If God so sanctified these means, who are we to deny ourselves or others the same privileges?

Would the book of Job or the Psalms be the same without imagination? Consider Psalm 23:

> *The LORD is my shepherd,*
> *I shall not want.*
> *He makes me lie down in green pastures;*
> *He leads me beside quiet waters.*
> *He restores my soul;*
> *He guides me in the paths of righteousness*
> *For His name's sake.*
> *Even though I walk through the valley of*
> *the shadow of death,*
>
> *I fear no evil; for Thou art with me;*
> *Thy rod and Thy staff, they comfort me.*

Thou dost prepare a table before me in the
presence of my enemies;
Thou hast anointed my head with oil;
My cup overflows.
Surely goodness and lovingkindness will
follow me all the days of my life,
And I will dwell in the house of the LORD *forever.*

The whole truth of this psalm could be stated in simple, abstract terms: The LORD God will take care of His people both now and in the life to come! Yet how much more powerful, more comforting, more memorable, and more enduring is the imaginative reproduction of the Divine Author?

The prophets spoke with imagination, and so with power. Who cannot read these awesome prophecies and not be moved by the grandeur of their divine pronouncements? Isaiah's indictment of Israel (1:2–3) must be read, for it cannot be explained:

Listen, O heavens, and hear, O earth;
For the LORD *speaks,*
"Sons I have reared and brought up,
But they have revolted against Me.
An ox knows its owner,
And a donkey its master's manger,
But Israel does not know,
My people do not understand."

The power of Isaiah's preaching is not only in what he said but also in how he said it. In Isaiah you see the majestic holiness of God described (chap. 6), the hope of Israel dramatically presented (chap. 40), the Suffering Servant sorrowfully depicted (chap. 53), and the millennial blessing beautifully portrayed (chap. 56). The other prophets follow the same pattern. Truth is powerfully presented in concrete terms. Grand themes are robed in the royal garb of humanity's finest means of expression. Mean words are for mean things. Majestic words are used for majestic things. In the Word of God we are forced to deal with the eternal, the holy, the sublime, and the awesome, and we dare not array them with the pauper's rag of abstraction or the black sackcloth of dullness.

In the New Testament we meet the same imaginative style as in the Old Testament. The Gospels are narratives! We do not read the gospel; we see it, we feel it, we hear it, and so we are made to believe it. Fully half of the New Testament is narrative, and it is so for a purpose. Just as a picture is worth a thousand words, so narrative is worth a thousand sermons in prose!

Look at the preachers of the New Testament. John the Baptist was powerful for more than one reason. He was chosen and anointed. He was filled with the Spirit. He was bold and courageous. He was dedicated and austere, a man of God and not a man of this world. Yet to all this can be added that he was imaginative. He preached the concrete. His sermons were full of descriptive terms and devices.

- *As to his person,* he was "the voice of one crying in the wilderness, 'Make ready the way of the Lord, make His paths straight'" (Matt. 3:3).
- *As to his preaching,* "Repent, for the kingdom of heaven is at hand" (Matt. 3:2).
- *As to his indictment of hypocrites,* "You brood of vipers, who warned you to flee from the wrath to come?" (Matt. 3:7).
- *As to his warnings,* "The ax is already laid at the root of the trees; every tree therefore that does not bear good fruit is cut down and thrown into the fire" (Matt. 3:10).
- *As to his humility,* "but He who is coming after me is mightier than I, and I am not fit to remove His sandals" (Matt. 3:11).
- *As to his descriptions of the Messiah,* "He Himself will baptize you with the Holy Spirit and fire. And His winnowing fork is in His hand, and He will thoroughly clean His threshing floor; and He will gather His wheat into the barn, but He will burn up the chaff with unquenchable fire" (Matt. 3:11–12).

The Lord Jesus Himself is the Master Teacher. We learn from Him best how to teach and preach. The Holy Spirit has seen fit to give us an ample supply of examples through Him on how to teach and preach with imagination. We have both His extended sermons and His short, pithy statements. In the Gospels we see Christ make use of a variety of communicative tools current in His day. They are there to be studied and to be used for our own preaching, carefully modified to speak to our own world, just as He spoke to His.

Our Lord was an effective communicator, and not just because He was God or because of His miracles. He was also a great teacher. White says,

> What drew the crowds to Christ was that He spoke the language of the people with vivid concreteness, never in abstract terms; and that He spoke "from their floor level." Jesus was interested in their problems, but as His words show, He was interested also in their homes, fishing, sowing, marketing, family life, bread-making, wine-brewing, patching garments, shepherding—and all the rest.[10]

Take a Gospel journey with Christ and you will see the truthfulness of the previous assessment. Read the Sermon on the Mount and isolate in detail the devices that make the sermon "the greatest sermon ever preached!" Every sentence is full of imagination, of description, of concreteness, and of clarity. No wonder the crowds were "amazed at His teaching" (Matt. 7:28). Listen to His teaching with parables, and never be content to teach without one (cf. Matt. 13, 20, 25). See His righteous indignation vented on the religious leaders in unparalleled descriptive terms. Sit and listen to the vision of the future—both of Jerusalem and of the world—in the Olivet discourse, and never live a day without the thought of His soon return as "a thief in the night." Even the visit to Gethsemane and Golgotha will impress you with how Jesus not only lived but also died with imagination. The vacant cross and the empty tomb are both symbols of victory, and planned symbols they are!

The great preachers of the past and present are all imitators of the Master Teacher. They are word-craftsmen who—on the anvil of heart and study—worked hard to present God's Word in a clear and moving manner. Their imitation of the Master and their creative labors repaid them greatly, and the church is richer because of them. May we follow in their train!

Tools for Imaginative Preaching

All preaching can be improved. In fact, preaching needs to be constantly adapting itself to the changing face of culture. The message will never change, but the way we deliver it will change—yes, *must change*—or we will cease to be a bridge between two worlds (to borrow from John Stott's expression). Here I will list four tools that will help us to be more imaginative and, hence, more passionate, in our preaching.

> ### Tools for Imaginative Preaching
>
> ▶ Power words
> ▶ Figures of speech
> ▶ Illustrations
> ▶ Stories

1. *Power words*. Words are the building blocks of ideas and ultimately of sermons. Every preacher is a wordsmith. He deals in words! Words are the vehicles of thought, and what words we choose to use will determine the ultimate effect our sermons will have on the audience. We have choices when it comes to words, and we should make it a point to choose words that appeal to our senses: "Words that appeal to the five senses—sight, touch, smell, taste, and hearing—will help people sense what you are saying, understand it better, and remember it longer."[11] Hence, choose words that describe, that picture exactly what you see and feel and hear! Try not to approximate. Look for exactly the right word, and ensure that it's the word your audience has in mind.

Choose nouns and verbs above adjectives and adverbs. Robinson says, "Vividness develops when we let nouns and verbs carry our meaning. Adjectives and adverbs clutter speech and keep company with weak words. . . . Strong nouns and verbs stand alone."[12] Keep in mind that the spoken word and the written word are different. The spoken word must appeal to both the ear and the eye.

2. *Figures of speech.* Powerful preaching looks for powerful ways to present the truth. Powerful preaching is that which arrests the attention of the listener, carries him away from any distraction, and, when the preacher is done with him, leaves an indelible mark upon his soul. Hence, we look for all of those devices that help us accomplish just that. Human speech has created such a variety of means to express ideas. These we call *figures of speech.* Broadus states on the use of figures of speech,

> Perhaps the chief element of energy in style is the use of figures of speech. Passionate feeling, whether anger, fear, love, or the emotion of the sublime, naturally expresses itself by means of bold imagery. . . . Figures usually contribute to elegance of style, and some of them—comparison especially—to perspicuity; but their most considerable aid is in matter of energy.[13]

If we are to be passionate and earnest in our preaching, we must make studied and purposeful use of these figures of speech in our preaching. Let us examine a few of them.

> *Metaphor* is a figure of speech that instead of comparing one thing with another, one identifies the two by taking the name or assuming the attributes of the one for the other.[14] Our Lord made ample use of metaphors:
>
> - "You are the salt of the earth" (Matt. 5:13).
> - "Do not be afraid, little flock" (Luke 12:32).
> - "I am the door" (John 10:9).
>
> In metaphors, we substitute a word or figure that opens upon a familiar truth to which we may compare a new idea, yet we do so with a great economy of words. The key to using metaphors is to ensure that they reveal and do not conceal or

distract from the comparison. Overused metaphors—or worse, mixed metaphors—will respectively dull or confuse.

Synecdoche is a figure of speech in which a part of a thing is taken for a whole and thus may be more expressive:

- "They will hammer their swords into plowshares, and their spears into pruning hooks" (Isa. 2:4).
- "For you are dust, and to dust you shall return" (Gen. 3:19).
- ". . . to bring them up from that land to a good and spacious land, to a land flowing with milk and honey" (Exod. 3:8).
- "For I will not trust in my bow, nor will my sword save me" (Ps. 44:6).

Hyperbole is saying more than what is meant! This is also called "exaggeration" and can be used with great effect when the preacher shows strong feelings toward something or someone. Consider these examples:

- "If your right eye makes you stumble, tear it out, and throw it from you; for it is better for you that one of the parts of your body perish, than for your whole body to be thrown into hell" (Matt. 5:29).
- "How can you say to your brother, 'Let me take the speck out of your eye,' and behold, the log is in your own eye?" (Matt. 7:4).
- "It is easier for a camel to go through the eye of a needle, than for a rich man to enter the kingdom of God" (Matt. 19:24).

Personification ascribes personal qualities, actions, and speech to inanimate things.[15] Solomon personified wisdom in the book of Proverbs, and Paul did the same with love in 1 Corinthians 13. Other examples include the following:

- "Lift up your heads, O gates, and be lifted up, O ancient doors, that the King of glory may come in!" (Ps. 24:7).
- "Listen, O heavens, and hear, O earth; for the LORD speaks" (Isa. 1:2).

Apostrophe is the device of turning from the audience to address a person or a thing. Jesus turned to Jerusalem and emotionally cried out, "O Jerusalem, Jerusalem . . ." We can see how emotions would use this figure of speech, for emotions often interrupt our more regular patterns of speech. See Jeremiah 2:12–13 for its effect!

Exclamation is quite naturally the result of strong emotion. "God forbid," "Alas," or "Woe is me!" are all proper uses of exclamation.

Interrogation is the act of asking a question either to a third party, a supposed antagonist, or to the audience itself. Here is a device that increases attention and can surely arouse the emotions. The book of Malachi and Galatians 3:1–5 provide excellent examples of this figure of speech.

Dramatism was used effectively by the prophets to drive home their message (cf. Jer. 4:19). We may act out the part we are preaching. When done well, it has great effect.

Naturally, the student of preaching will want to go deeper into the use and variety of figures of speech. The study of rhetoric will repay you immensely!

Figures of speech can also add beauty to a sermon when used with great care and imagination. Consider this:

Imagination rejoices in tropes and figures. She trails the ornamental epithet round the bare substantive as the gardener trails the ivy round the pillar. She loves to speed home her thought by climax and antithesis. She cultivates the figures of simile and metaphor in order to shed new light upon old truths, comparing spiritual with natural and natural with spiritual things. Not content with these, she goes on from metaphor to allegory, expanding the chosen figure in more intimate and loving detail (compare the Song of the Vineyard in Isa. 5 or the Good Shepherd in John 10). Or she apostrophizes and personifies, breathing life into the inanimate and a personal soul into the inorganic (compare the personification of Wisdom in Proverbs). She sits down and spins a parable to illustrate religious or moral truths by the happenings of every day. For she is the sworn foe of the abstract and must present everything in forms of concrete reality. She desires to catch the eye of the hearer as well as his ear; the one is to assist the other, so that the discourse may be doubly sure to attain its goal. Thus the spoken word becomes in her hand, as it were, a painter's brush with which she imparts outline and color to the inmost thoughts and feelings of the heart.[16]

Therefore, do not be afraid to use figures of speech. As one writer has noted, "although figures can be overused, misused, or used in a self-serving way, most preachers, it seems, fail to tap their potential. Figures serve a good purpose."[17]

3. *Illustrations*. Passionate preaching must have light as well as heat. The preacher must explain as well as apply. Hence, there exists the need to illustrate, to add light to the subject. Illustrations are the windows to the discourse—they shed light on the subject being discussed. Michael Green, in his preface to his book, *Illustrations for Biblical Preaching*, states,

Sermon illustrations are like color on a car. Although they are no substitute for careful study and exposition of the text, they do make its presentation more interesting. In addition, like a flashing red light in your rear-view mirror, they can arrest attention. And they can ignite a response as quickly as a lightening bolt in a drought-stricken land.[18]

Illustrations serve many purposes. Richard Mayhue offers the following *whys* of illustrating:

1. to interest the mind and secure the continuing attention of the audience;
2. to make preaching three dimensional and lifelike;
3. to explain Christian doctrine and duties clearly and understandably;
4. to communicate convincingly to those who respond better to pictures than to facts;
5. to ensure that the message is unforgettable;
6. to involve the human senses in the communication process; and
7. to catch the hearing of the disinterested.[19]

Spurgeon states that illustrations help to enliven an audience and quicken their attention.[20] The proper use of illustrations can greatly aid the sermon in provoking an audience to action. Spurgeon adds this chastisement:

> Those who are accustomed to the soporific sermonizing of certain dignified divines would marvel greatly if they could see the enthusiasm and lively delight with which congregations listen to speech through which there flows a quiet current of happy, natural illustrations.[21]

R. O. White concurs:

> It is true that a certain kind of intellectual snobbery affects to disparage illustration, as needed only by untrained minds. A certain type of spiritual self-righteousness, too, sometimes pretends that a scriptural message, filled with sound doctrine, needs no titivating with engaging stories. Usually, those who so contend speak more than they listen: frequent listeners would never talk such nonsense.[22]

What would the ministry of Christ have been without the art of illustration? Mark noted that He "was not speaking to them without parables" (Mark 4:34). The power of illustration is vividly portrayed in the parable of the Good Samaritan (Luke 10:30–37) and in the parable of the Prodigal Son (Luke 15:11–32). If you desire to be a powerful preacher, then make use of powerful illustrations. Use them often, but use them wisely.

Every preacher should have a method for finding and organizing illustrations. We need to be like that scribe who "brings forth out of his treasure things new and old" (Matt. 13:52). My personal "treasures" for illustrations are the Bible and life. I read the Bible with the expressed purpose of finding illustrations that will assist me in communicating the text (cf. 1 Cor. 10:11). Everyday life also contains innumerable illustrations from personal experiences, current events, books, newspaper articles, periodicals, and even television.

I file illustrations in three archives. One archive contains illustrations arranged according to specific topics or themes. A second archive contains illustrations grouped according to the books of the Bible— each one tagged to its specific passage. The third archive is an open file in which I keep the most current illustrations. Having easy access to a photocopier is a great help not only in saving an illustration but also for making multiple copies in case one needs to be filed in all three archives. Ultimately, the key is in finding a system that works for you.

4. *Stories.* A story is an "extended illustration." I set it apart from an "illustration" because a story is a "mini-sermon" with a single punch! A story is a personal anecdote about a person or persons that will help you to illustrate and apply truth. Calvin Miller says that "sermons without any stories translate as cold as the black tungsten filament of projector bulbs."[23] He adds,

> Ultimate stories tell of life truths, truths that are so filled with universal truth that they can speak to the smaller, particular truths of our hearts. Our members enter our churches with broken hearts; their life stories aren't working out. These attend us, filtering our sermons through their crying needs.

Dare we try to cure such pain with stories? For the person having a baby out of wedlock, or the child abuser, or the cancer victim, our sermons must tell deeply serious stories that relate, encircle, and save.[24]

Even the great Spurgeon was an advocate of stories. Hear him again:

> It ought never be forgotten that the great God Himself, when He would instruct men, employs histories and biographies. Our Bible contains doctrines, promises, and precepts; but these are not left alone, the whole book is vivified and illustrated by marvelous records of things said and done by God and by men. He who is taught of God values the sacred histories, and knows that in them there is a special fullness and forcibleness of instruction. Teachers of Scripture cannot do better than instruct their fellows after the manner of the Scriptures.[25]

So, my fellow preachers, tell stories, biblical stories, personal stories, biographical stories, and even hypothetical stories. Tell them powerfully, and they will aid in your preaching passionately and persuasively. Remember, Nathan converted David with a story, and Jesus Himself moved His audience and condemned His foes with stories.

Essentials in Imaginative Preaching

In closing this chapter on preaching with imagination, I wish to spur you to the development of this facet of preaching by considering certain essentials to keep in mind. Although all men are born with imagination, not all of us cultivate this capacity to the point that it does anyone any good. If we are to grow as preachers, we need to cultivate our ability to think and preach with imagination. White affirms,

> It is of course true that imagination varies in different men; but as a natural capacity distinctive of the human mind it is capable of development, of exercise and growth. For this reason we speak of the cultivation of imagination, and the

development facility of illustration, as part of the continuing discipline of the preacher eager to grow even better at his task.[26]

If we would grow in this dimension, we must keep the following four essentials in mind:

Four Essentials for Preaching with Imagination

- ▶ Gain freedom from fear.
- ▶ Seek liberty in preaching.
- ▶ Learn to rethink imaginatively.
- ▶ Practice imaginative preaching.

1. *Gain freedom from fear.* Imaginative preaching may be confused with sermons artificially charged with emotion. True, there are those who play to the emotions, who try to manipulate an audience by emotional appeals and stirring stories. But such should not rob you of the use of imagination in preaching, just as the charlatans of Paul's day did not diminish his use of rhetoric to accomplish the proper end of the gospel.

True imaginative preaching naturally creates emotion because the preacher is already genuinely overcome by the truth he intends to convey. Do not be ashamed or afraid of your emotions. If others would criticize you for being too emotional, too imaginative, or too earthly in your preaching, consider it a compliment rather than a criticism. Remember that an energetic style proceeds from an energetic nature!

2. *Seek liberty in preaching.* We err by holding ourselves to the artificial ruler of homiletics that hinders creativity and imagination. The whole essence of preaching is to *be yourself!* The eagle will fly highest when it learns to harness the wind and to let go of the branch upon which it perches. Sadly, we learn preaching from books or from those who cannot preach. We should make it our goal to learn preaching from those who are set free to communicate passionately what God has given them. We need to cast off someone else's armor, as David did Saul's, and we must preach with the sling and stones in sync with our emotions.

Recognize that passion has an order of itself. Passionate living teaches us to trust our instincts, and such living often defies logic. Man first acts, then he creates rules of conduct. Keep this principle in mind when seeking to preach with imagination.

3. *Learn to rethink imaginatively.* Scholarship tends to turn our thinking abstract—things become only black or white. Whether it is books, the nature of lectureship, or the impatience with emotional learning, we can become guilty of being abstract preachers. Yet nature and everyday life team with imagination like the colors of the rainbow. We do not normally live our everyday lives in the abstract. Hence, think colors and concrete pictures, and people will not only understand more fully but also be delighted by the truth they see.

We must learn to paint pictures with words. When my children were growing, I would ask them to lie on the floor with me, to close their eyes, and listen to a story I had prepared for them. Then I, too, would close my eyes and proceed to tell the story, drawing verbal pictures to inspire their imaginations. This proved to be an excellent exercise for me, and it became a favorite part of the week for them!

4. *Practice imaginative preaching.* For some reason, preachers hardly ever practice their preaching. What I mean is that although we do a lot of preaching and public speaking, very few of us make a concentrated and consistent effort to improve our preaching skills. We think a two-semester course in seminary is enough to make us modern-day Chrysostoms or Spurgeons. But preaching is a complicated art, involving the use of many muscles as well as the coordination of mind and body, of both preacher and audience. It is not easily mastered.

Have you noticed that all other professions take training and practice to bring about excellence, especially those that involve the use of words to address an audience, such as music, drama, acting, and other types of public discourse? The musicians learn their scales, the soloist learns her parts, and the artist learns brush strokes to aid him in his delivery. Is the preacher any different? Then why do we not practice our preaching? Why do we not print a manuscript of our sermon and then practice it? Why do we not seek to better our preaching by a conscious effort?

Regardless of your answer, I trust that you see the logic behind this reasoning. Preaching with imagination takes study, practice, hard work, and, above all, diligence. If we wish to be powerful, passionate preachers, we must learn to preach with imagination, and that will entail practice.

May God bless your labors!

Conclusion

So shall My word be which goes forth from My mouth; it shall not return to Me empty, without accomplishing what I desire, and without succeeding in the matter for which I sent it.
—Isaiah 55:11

I believe in preaching—*expository preaching* to be exact. Moreover, I believe that the Bible is the inerrant, authoritative Word of God, containing all that mankind needs for salvation and sanctification. I also believe that the preaching of the Word is the God-ordained method of communicating God's truth to this world and to His church. Hence, I am bullish about preaching!

I also believe in preaching with passion. Some people say that I am passionate because of my Latin heritage. Actually, I am passionate because God's Word makes me so and because man's condition demands it. Ultimately, the nature of preaching deserves it.

Expository preaching is also my passion. The systematic exposition of the books of the Bible is the key to comprehending fully the "whole counsel of God," both for the preacher and for the church. Unfortunately, most of what is called "expository preaching" today is nothing more than the sharing of exegetical insights or a running commentary on a book of the Bible. The average believer is consequently being inoculated against such a splendid and profitable means of preaching. What is needed in the "exegesis" is an understanding of the ultimate purpose of preaching. Then the sermon needs to be delivered passionately. The purpose of this book is to help us preach the "Book" passionately. People will come to a church service not because we have gimmicks and games to attract them, but because the Word of God goes forth with power through a man who is "white-hot" for God and His purposes.

> *"I am passionate because God's Word makes me so, because man's condition demands it, and ultimately, because the nature of preaching deserves it."*

When Luther included secular rhythms in his hymnology, he said, "Why should Satan have all the good music?" I echo the same for preaching: Why should the Devil have all the great communicators? Preachers, we have the truth! We have God's Word! We have the mandate to preach the Word! Why not preach it passionately and powerfully? The future of the church depends on it! The lives of our listeners lie in the balance, which hangs on our preaching!

My prayer is that these few insights into preaching may transform your preaching and its effect upon your congregation and, ultimately, the world. If there is but a small measure of change in your pulpit, I will have considered my labor repaid beyond measure.

I close with a searching quotation from my favorite preacher of old, Charles Spurgeon:

> How shall we describe the doom of an unfaithful minister? And every unearnest minister is unfaithful. I would infinitely prefer to be consigned to Tophet as a murderer of men's bodies than as a destroyer of men's souls; neither do I know of any condition in which a man can perish so fatally, so infinitely, as in that of the man who preaches a gospel which he does not believe, and assumes the office of pastor over a people whose good he does not intensely desire. Let us pray to be found faithful always, and ever. God grant that the Holy Spirit may make and keep us so.[1]

Amen.

Endnotes

Introduction

1. My conviction is that the leadership role of the pastor is reserved for men only. Hence, the preacher of the Word will be a role almost exclusively reserved for men, although God will use gifted women to speak to other women. For the sake of simplicity, I will use the male gender in referring to the preacher.
2. Jerry Vines, *A Guide to Effective Sermon Delivery* (Chicago: Moody, 1986), 148.
3. D. Martyn Lloyd-Jones, *Preaching and Preachers* (Grand Rapids: Zondervan, 1971), 93.
4. Geoffry Thomas, "Powerful Preaching," in *The Preacher and Preaching,* ed. Samuel Logan (Phillipsburg, N.J.: Presbyterian and Reformed, 1986), 369.
5. W. A. Criswell, *Criswell's Guidebook for Pastors* (Nashville: Broadman & Holman, 1980), 58.
6. Ibid., 54.
7. Lloyd-Jones, *Preaching and Preachers,* 97.
8. Charles H. Spurgeon, *Lectures to My Students* (Grand Rapids: Zondervan, 1954), 307.
9. Lloyd-Jones, *Preaching and Preachers,* 87.
10. John Broadus, *On the Preparation and Delivery of Sermons* (New York: Harper & Row, 1944), 252–53.

Chapter 1

1. David L. Larsen, *The Company of Preachers* (Grand Rapids: Kregel, 1998), 159.
2. Stephen F. Olford, *Anointed Expository Preaching* (Nashville: Broadman & Holman, 1998), 44.
3. Ibid., 21.
4. Michael Duduit, *Communicate with Power* (Grand Rapids: Baker, 1996), 223.
5. Richard Baxter, *The Reformed Pastor* (Edinburgh: Banner of Truth Trust, 1974), 61–63.
6. D. Martin Lloyd-Jones, *Preaching and Preachers* (Grand Rapids: Zondervan, 1971), 172.
7. Charles Bridges, *The Christian Ministry* (Edinburgh: Banner of Truth Trust, 1967), 147.
8. Charles H. Spurgeon, *Lectures to My Students* (Grand Rapids: Zondervan, 1954), 45.
9. Bridges, *Christian Ministry*, 91.
10. Spurgeon, *Lectures to My Students*, 25.
11. W. H. Griffith-Thomas, *Ministerial Life and Work* (Grand Rapids: Baker, 1974), 93.
12. Lloyd-Jones, *Preaching and Preachers*, 103.
13. Ibid., 107.
14. John F. MacArthur Jr., "The Highest Calling" (an invocation message at The Master's Seminary, Sun Valley, Calif., 9 September 1990).
15. Tony Sargent, *The Sacred Anointing* (Wheaton, Ill.: Crossway, 1994), 59.
16. Ibid., 59–64.
17. Ibid., 64.
18. Olford, *Anointed Expository Preaching*, 217.
19. W. E. Sangster, *Power in Preaching* (New York: Abingdon, 1958), 106.
20. Susannah Spurgeon and Joseph Harrald, eds., *C. H. Spurgeon Autobiography*, vol. 2, *The Full Harvest: 1860–1892* (Edinburgh: Banner of Truth Trust, 1973), 327–28.

Chapter 2

1. Roy B. Zuck, *The Speaker's Quote Book* (Grand Rapids: Kregel, 1997), 88.
2. *Funk and Wagnalls Standard Desk Dictionary* (New York: Funk & Wagnalls, 1969), 140.
3. W. E. Sangster, *Power in Preaching* (New York: Abingdon, 1958), 31.
4. John F. MacArthur Jr., "About the Master's Seminary," http://www.mastersem.edu/tmsad.htm; INTERNET.

5. Gardiner Spring, *The Power in the Pulpit* (Edinburgh: The Banner of Truth Trust, 1986), 132.
6. Sangster, *Power in Preaching*, 40.

Chapter 3

1. D. Martyn Lloyd-Jones, *Preaching and Preachers* (Grand Rapids: Zondervan, 1971), 92.
2. *Webster's Universal College Dictionary* (New York: Gramercy Books, 1997), 164.
3. G. Abbott-Smith, "σπλαγχνιζομαι," in *A Manual Greek Lexicon of the New Testament* (Edinburgh: T & T Clark, 1991), 414.
4. Richard Baxter, *The Reformed Pastor* (Edinburgh: Banner of Truth Trust, 1974), 197.
5. Charles H. Spurgeon, *Lectures to My Students* (Grand Rapids: Zondervan, 1954), 307.
6. Ibid., 307.
7. Baxter, *Reformed Pastor*, 199.

Chapter 4

1. William Hendriksen, *Exposition of the Gospel According to Matthew*, in *New Testament Commentary* (Grand Rapids: Baker, 1973), 382–83.
2. R. C. H. Lenski, *The Interpretation of St. Matthew's Gospel* (Minneapolis: Augsburg, 1943), 314.
3. F. W. Farrar, quoted in Lenski, *Matthew*, 315.
4. John Broadus, *Commentary on Matthew* (Grand Rapids: Kregel, 1990), 172.
5. *Webster's Universal College Dictionary* (New York: Gramercy Books, 1997), 53.
6. D. Martyn Lloyd-Jones, *Preaching and Preachers* (Grand Rapids: Zondervan, 1971), 83.
7. John Maxwell, *Developing the Leader Within You* (Nashville, Tenn.: Nelson, 1993), 12.
8. Ibid.
9. James Cox, *Preaching* (San Francisco: Harper & Row, 1988), 21.
10. Timothy A. Turner, *Preaching to Programmed People* (Grand Rapids: Kregel, 1995), 16.

Chapter 5

1. *Webster's Universal College Dictionary* (New York: Gramercy Books, 1997), 865.
2. David Eby, *Power Preaching for Church Growth* (Fearn, Great Britain: Mentor, 1996), 49.

3. Ibid., 52.
4. Richard Baxter, *The Reformed Pastor* (Edinburgh: Banner of Truth Trust, 1974), 70.
5. D. Martyn Lloyd-Jones, *Preaching and Preachers* (Grand Rapids: Zondervan, 1971), 91.
6. Charles H. Spurgeon, *Lectures to My Students* (Grand Rapids: Zondervan, 1954), 308–309.
7. Lloyd-Jones, *Preaching and Preachers*, 91–92.
8. Jerry Vines, *A Guide to Effective Sermon Delivery* (Chicago: Moody, 1986), 152.
9. Baxter, *Reformed Pastor*, 121.
10. David L. Larsen, *The Company of Preachers* (Grand Rapids: Kregel, 1998), 282.
11. Baxter, *Reformed Pastor*, 148–49.
12. Larsen, *Company of Preachers*, 374.
13. Baxter, *Reformed Pastor*, 149.

Chapter 6

1. In Stephen Olford, *Anointed Expository Preaching* (Nashville: Broadman & Holman, 1998), 44.
2. Roy B. Zuck, *The Speaker's Quote Book* (Grand Rapids: Kregel, 1997), 305.
3. Jerry Vines, *A Guide to Effective Sermon Delivery* (Chicago: Moody, 1986), 155.
4. *Webster's Universal College Dictionary* (New York: Gramercy Books, 1997), 101.

Chapter 7

1. H. C. Brown, *Steps to the Sermon* (Nashville: Broadman & Holman, 1996), 189.
2. Richard Baxter, *The Reformed Pastor* (Edinburgh: Banner of Truth Trust, 1974), 149.
3. Al Fasol, *A Complete Guide to Sermon Delivery* (Nashville: Broadman & Holman, 1996), 73.
4. *Webster's Universal College Dictionary* (New York: Gramercy Books, 1997), 340.
5. Jerry Vines, *A Guide to Effective Sermon Delivery* (Chicago: Moody, 1986), 151–52.
6. Stephen Olford, *Anointed Expository Preaching* (Nashville: Broadman & Holman, 1998), 204.
7. Haddon Robinson, *Biblical Preaching* (Grand Rapids: Baker, 1980), 201.
8. Vines, *Effective Sermon Delivery*, 139.

9. Olford, *Anointed Expository Preaching*, 205.
10. Brown, *Steps to the Sermon*, 208.
11. John A. Broadus, *On the Preparation and Delivery of Sermons* (New York: Harper & Row, 1944), 347.
12. Charles H. Spurgeon, *Lectures to My Students* (Grand Rapids: Zondervan, 1954), 118.
13. Broadus, *Preparation and Delivery of Sermons*, 347.
14. Brown, *Steps to the Sermon*, 203.
15. Broadus, *Preparation and Delivery of Sermons*, 354.
16. Fasol, *Guide to Sermon Delivery*, 82.
17. Vines, *Effective Sermon Delivery*, 140–41.
18. Broadus, *Preparation and Delivery of Sermons*, 355.
19. Brown, *Steps to the Sermon*, 204.
20. Vines, *Effective Sermon Delivery*, 143.

Chapter 8

1. Calvin Miller, *Spirit, Word, and Story* (Dallas: Word, 1989), 113.
2. *Webster's Universal College Dictionary* (New York: Gramercy Books, 1997), 407.
3. Michael Duduit, *Communicate with Power* (Grand Rapids: Baker, 1996), 210.
4. See the concise definition in John F. MacArthur Jr., "Rediscovering Expository Preaching," in *Rediscovering Expository Preaching* (Dallas: Word, 1992), 11.
5. John F. MacArthur Jr., "Frequently Asked Questions About Expository Preaching," in *Rediscovering Expository Preaching*, 343–44.
6. R. E. D. White, *A Guide to Preaching* (Grand Rapids: Eerdmans, 1973), 159.
7. Ibid., 158.
8. Warren Wiersbe, *Preaching and Teaching with Imagination* (Wheaton, Ill.: Victor Books, 1994), 36.
9. White, *A Guide to Preaching*, 161.
10. Ibid.
11. Bruce Mawhinney, *Preaching with Freshness* (Eugene, Ore.: Harvest House, 1991), 178.
12. Haddon Robinson, *Biblical Preaching* (Grand Rapids: Baker, 1980), 186.
13. John A. Broadus, *On the Preparation and Delivery of Sermons* (New York: Harper & Row, 1944), 263.
14. Ibid.
15. White, *A Guide to Preaching*, 215.
16. M. Reu, *Homiletics* (Grand Rapids: Baker, 1967), 193–94.
17. William H. Koolenga, *Elements of Style for Preaching* (Grand Rapids: Zondervan, 1989), 93.

18. Michael P. Green, *Illustrations for Biblical Preaching* (Grand Rapids: Baker, 1989), 9.
19. Richard Mayhue, "Introductions, Illustrations, and Conclusions," in *Rediscovering Expository Preaching*, 246.
20. Charles H. Spurgeon, *Lectures to My Students* (Grand Rapids: Zondervan, 1954), 351.
21. Ibid.
22. White, *A Guide to Preaching*, 171.
23. Miller, *Spirit, Word, and Story*, 148.
24. Ibid., 158.
25. Spurgeon, *Lectures to My Students*, 363.
26. White, *A Guide to Preaching*, 162.

Conclusion

1. Charles H. Spurgeon, *Lectures to My Students* (Grand Rapids: Zondervan, 1954), 320.

Bibliography

Abbott-Smith, G. *A Manual Greek Lexicon of the New Testament*. Edinburgh: T & T Clark, 1991.

Baxter, Richard. *The Reformed Pastor*. Edinburgh: Banner of Truth Trust, 1974.

Bridges, Charles. *The Christian Ministry*. Edinburgh: Banner of Truth Trust, 1967.

Broadus, John. *Commentary on Matthew*. Grand Rapids: Kregel, 1990.

———. *On the Preparation and Delivery of Sermons*. New York: Harper & Row Publishers, 1944.

Brown, H. C. *Steps to the Sermon*. Nashville: Broadman & Holman, 1996.

Criswell, W. A. *Criswell's Guidebook for Pastors*. Nashville: Broadman & Holman, 1980.

Cox, James. *Preaching*. San Fransisco: Harper & Row, 1988.

Duduit, Michael. *Communicate with Power*. Grand Rapids: Baker, 1996.

Eby, David. *Power Preaching for Church Growth*. Fearn, Great Britain: Mentor, 1996.

Fasol, Al. *A Complete Guide to Sermon Delivery*. Nashville: Broadman & Holman, 1996.

Funk and Wagnalls Standard Desk Dictionary. New York: Funk & Wagnalls, 1969.

Green, Michael P. *Illustrations for Biblical Preaching*. Grand Rapids: Baker, 1989.

Griffith-Thomas, W. H. *Ministerial Life and Work*. Grand Rapids: Baker, 1974.

Hendriksen, William. *Exposition of the Gospel According to Matthew*. In *New Testament Commentary*. Grand Rapids: Baker, 1873.

Koolenga, William H. *Elements of Style for Preaching.* Grand Rapids: Zondervan, 1989.

Larsen, David L. *The Company of Preachers.* Grand Rapids: Kregel, 1998.

Lenski, R. C. H. *The Interpretation of St. Matthew's Gospel.* Minneapolis: Augsburg, 1943.

Lloyd-Jones, D. Martyn. *Preaching and Preachers.* Grand Rapids: Zondervan, 1971.

MacArthur, John F., Jr. "About the Master's Seminary." Http://www.mastersem.edu/tmsad.htm.

———. "The Highest Calling." An invocation message at the Master's Seminary, Sun Valley, Calif., 9 September 1990.

MacArthur, John F., Jr., et al. *Rediscovering Expository Preaching.* Dallas: Word, 1992.

Mawhinney, Bruce. *Preaching with Freshness.* Eugene, Ore.: Harvest House, 1991.

Maxwell, John. *Developing the Leader Within You.* Nashville: Nelson, 1993.

Miller, Calvin. *Spirit, Word, and Story.* Dallas: Word, 1989.

Olford, Stephen F. *Anointed Expository Preaching.* Nashville: Broadman & Holman, 1988.

Reu, M. *Homiletics.* Grand Rapids: Baker, 1967.

Robinson, Haddon. *Biblical Preaching.* Grand Rapids: Baker, 1980.

Sangster, W. E. *Power in Preaching.* New York: Abingdon, 1958.

Sargent, Tony. *The Sacred Anointing.* Wheaton: Crossway, 1994.

Spring, Gardiner. *The Power in the Pulpit.* Edinburgh: Banner of Truth Trust, 1986.

Spurgeon, Charles H. *Lectures to My Students.* Grand Rapids: Zondervan, 1954.

Spurgeon, Susannah, and Joseph Harrald, eds. *C. H. Spurgeon Autobiography.* Vol. 2, *The Full Harvest: 1860–1892.* Edinburgh, Banner of Truth Trust.

Thomas, Geoffry. "Powerful Preaching." In *The Preacher and Preaching.* Ed. Samuel Logan. Phillipsburg, N.J.: Presbyterian and Reformed, 1986.

Turner, Timothy. *Preaching to Programmed People.* Grand Rapids: Kregel, 1995.

Vines, Jerry. *A Guide to Effective Sermon Delivery.* Chicago: Moody, 1986.

Webster's Universal College Dictionary. New York: Gramercy Books, 1997.

White, R. E. D. *A Guide to Preaching.* Grand Rapids: Eerdmans, 1973.

Wiersbe, Warren. *Preaching and Teaching with Imagination.* Wheaton: Victor Books, 1994.

Zuck, Roy B. *The Speaker's Quote Book.* Grand Rapids: Kregel, 1997.